LOADED VEHICLES

Studies in African Literary Media

Bernth Lindfors

Africa World Press, Inc.

P.O. Box 1892

P.O. Box 48

Trenton, NJ 08607

Asmara, ERITREA

Africa World Press, Inc.

P.O. Box 1892
Trenton, NJ 08607

P.O. Box 48
Asmara, ERITREA

Copyright © 1996 Bernth Lindfors

First Printing 1996

Cover Design: Linda Nickens

Library of Congress Cataloging-in-Publication Data

Lindfors, Bernth.
    Loaded vehicles : studies in African literary media / Bernth
Lindfors.
        p.   cm.
    Includes bibliographical references and index.
    ISBN 0-86543-542-1 (cloth). --ISBN 0-86543-543-X (pbk.)
    1. African literature (English)--History and criticism.
2. Periodicals, Publishing of--Africa--History--20th century.
3. Literature--Publishing--Africa--History--20th century. 4. Books
and reading--Africa--History--20th century. 5. Mass media--Africa-
-History--20th century.   I. Title.
PR9340.5.L565   1996
820.9' 96--dc20
                                                96-16371
                                                    CIP

Contents

Acknowledgements v

Introduction vii

Journals
The Short Happy Life of the South African
Short Story, 1951-1963 3
The Ascent and Decline of *Black Orpheus* 23
African Little Magazines 43
Armah's Achimota Writings 53

Book Publishing at Home and Abroad
Romances for the Office Worker: Aubrey
Kalitera and Malawi's White-Collar
Reading Public 73
Dennis Brutus, Texas Poet 91

Wordplay
Perverted Proverbs in Onitsha Chapbooks 107
All the News in Fits of Print: An
Examination of Nigerian
Newspaper Headlines 117

Documents
Fagunwa's Opinions on Fiction 137
Ogunde on Ogunde: Two
Autobiographical Statements 145
Rotimi and Soyinka at Unife:
A Newspaper Controversy 157

Contents, continued

Works Cited 185

Index 195

Acknowledgements

I am grateful to the editors of *African Book Publishing Record, Kiabàrà, Matatu, Nigerian Tribune, Phylon, Proverbium, Theatre Review* (formerly *Educational Theatre Review*), *Commonwealth: Essays and Studies*, and *World Literature Today* (formerly *Books Abroad*) and to the book editors of *European-Language Writing in Sub-Saharan Africa, Paisanos: A Folklore Miscellany, Major Minorities: English Literatures in Transit*, and *Critical Perspectives on Dennis Brutus* for permission to reprint material that first appeared in their pages. Every effort has been made to trace the owners of copyright to all lengthy quotations, but in a few cases this has proved impossible; I would like to hear from any who have been missed.

I also wish to express my gratitude to the University Research Institute at The University of Texas at Austin for providing funds for typesetting this book, and to Cinde Hastings for preparing the final camera-ready copy.

ntroduction

When comprehensive histories of modern African literatures come to be written, some attention will have to be given to ephemeral printed media that provided aspiring authors with opportunities to express themselves. In many parts of the continent, school and university publications, literary reviews, popular magazines, pamphlets and newspapers have helped to stimulate literary creativity by offering regular outlets for short fiction, poetry, drama, essays and reviews. Indeed, without the encouragement that these local vehicles afforded, it is unlikely that strong literary movements would have emerged as swiftly as they did in Nigeria, South Africa, Kenya, Ghana, Zimbabwe and Malawi, to name only the most conspicuous examples from anglophone Africa. Nearly all young writers in these nations got started by addressing their own countrymen in inexpensive media produced domestically. Only a few ventured to send their first manuscripts to publishers in Europe or America. The opening chapters of any African literary history must thus begin at home, not abroad.

And later chapters must take account of what lies buried in indigenous media instead of relying solely on documentation that is readily available internationally. Through this kind of archival archaeology Africa's forgotten literary history can be retrieved and put on record, supplementing what is already known. By digging deeply into the recoverable past, we can gain a better understanding of how African literatures evolved in the environments that nourished them.

The essays in this book are efforts at excavating selected sites in the available documentary record on anglophone African literatures. I begin by exploring the contents of two key literary periodicals (*Drum* in South Africa, *Black Orpheus* in Nigeria), continue by surveying the characteristics of a number of little magazines, and then home in on a single Ghanaian high school annual, *The Achimotan*, in order to examine the earliest writings of Ayi Kwei Armah. In the next section I turn to two contrasting examples of book publishing: that of Aubrey Kalitera, a popular novelist in Malawi who has typed, bound, published and peddled most of his own fiction; and that of Dennis Brutus, an exiled South African poet who has had to rely on British, American and Nigerian publishers because his writings have been banned in his homeland. The third section focuses on imaginative use of the English language by Nigerian pamphleteers and journalists, and the fourth section reprints revealing essays, reminiscences and arguments by five important Nigerian writers: the late D.O. Fagunwa and the late Hubert Ogunde, both of whom wrote in Yoruba; and Ola Rotimi, Kole Omotoso and Wole Soyinka, who write in English.

Virtually all the documents reproduced in these essays first saw light somewhere in Africa, in media crafted by and for Africans. Such media—serials, books, pamphlets, newspapers—have always been loaded with interesting material, much of which has escaped the attention of the outside world. Yet these vehicles have been among the most powerful driving forces in Africa's recent literary history. It is time that they were recognized as such.

Journals

The Short Happy Life of the South African Short Story, 1951–1963

In the early years of the apartheid era black South African journalists and schoolteachers began producing a remarkably lively literature in English, but nearly all of them chose to express themselves in a single literary form: the short story. Unlike their contemporaries in West Africa, they did not write novels, plays or volumes of poetry, and unlike their predecessors in South Africa who had written in African languages, they did not turn out folktales, homilies or religious allegories for use in mission schools. They also declined to write in Afrikaans. Instead, they elected to deal with contemporary life in South Africa in a medium that was readily accessible to their public and in a language that enabled them to reach the widest possible readership. As one commentator on urban life in South Africa put it, "The advertisement hoardings are in English. The pulp magazines are in English. The pop songs are in English, English is fame, English is money; English is the means by which the urban African feels himself a citizen of the world" (Anon. 1962: 572). A South African writer who expressed himself in Afrikaans or in an African language was a citizen of a much smaller world.

But why the preference for short stories? Several black South African writers in exile tried to explain this phenomenon, relating it to the peculiar environment in which the black writer was forced to operate. Ezekiel Mphahlele, speaking of the decades encompassing and following the second world war, said that "During the last twenty years the political, social climate of South Africa has been growing viciously difficult for a nonwhite to write in. It requires tremendous organization of one's mental and emotional faculties before one can write a poem or a novel or a play. This has become all but impossible" (1962: 186). Bloke Modisane agreed that environmental circumstances in South Africa were conducive to short story writing because they forced black writers to adopt a "short term morality": "They have to live from day to day. You don't know if the sun is going to shine tomorrow. Everything you do must be done today. Only today is important. You cannot budget for six months in order to write a novel. The short story, therefore, serves an urgent, immediate, intense, concentrated form of unburdening yourself—and you must unburden yourself" ("Short Story" 3). Mphahlele and Modisane were speaking from personal experience, for when living in South Africa, both had sought to unburden themselves in other literary forms but had found it impossible to do so (Cousins 38; Modisane, *Blame Me* 46).

But another exile, Lewis Nkosi, had a different explanation for the phenomenon. He felt that the writers themselves must share a portion of the blame for failing to create a more substantial literature: "Part of the reason [for the absence of lengthier works] is sheer sloth. Also, some magazines have employed such low standards of selection that beginning writers began to get the idea that one could detour from the long and dreary labor of good writing by bashing out a short story in a matter of a day or two and getting it published immediately" (October 1962: 6). The readiness of these writers to exploit easy opportunities for publication had a deleterious effect not only on the form but also on the content, style and quality of their writing.

One of the magazines Nkosi must have had in mind was *Drum*, originally called *African Drum*, a monthly magazine published in Johannesburg. Financed by a white South African, edited first by a white south African and then by an Englishman,[1] *African Drum* was started in 1951 as a magazine "for Africa and the Africans," a magazine aimed at "150,000,000 Bantu and Negro inhabitants of the continent whom we will attempt to reach for the first time in history with words that will express their thoughts, their impulses, their endeavors and, ultimately, their souls" (Editorial, 15 March 1951: 3). The contents of the first issues reveal what the white proprietor and white editors thought would best express the African. There were articles on tribal history, tribal music, famous chiefs, farming, religion, and sports. On the literary pages there were folktales, excerpts from Alan Paton's *Cry, the Beloved Country*, and romantic poems about Africa by African-American poets.

The first issues of *African Drum* did not sell well. When the proprietor and editors tried to find out why Africans weren't buying it, they were told by one dissatisfied reader, "Ag, why do you dish out that stuff, man?...Tribal music! Tribal history! Chiefs! We don't care about chiefs! Give us jazz and film stars, man! We want Duke Ellington, Satchmo, and hot dames! Yes, brother, anything American. You can cut out this junk about kraals and folktales and Basutos in blankets—forget it! You're just trying to keep us backward, that's what!" (Sampson 20). *African Drum* had misjudged its reading public. Within a year it was transformed to *Drum*, a magazine for urban Africans which contained feature articles on jazz, crime, boxing and beauty contests. Pretty girls began to appear on its cover. *Drum*'s sales rose quickly.

The fiction in *Drum* changed too. Gone were the folktales, the stories about witch doctors and farm laborers, the stories about tribal Africans in pastoral settings. Replacing them were stories about city life, love stories, gangster stories, boxing stories, serialized detective thrillers, and true confessions. In 1952 *Drum* started to sponsor an annual short story competition with a first prize of fifty pounds. This stimulated a great deal of literary activity not only in South Africa but in other parts of the continent as well. In its peak year, 1957, *Drum*'s short story competition drew manuscripts from 1,638 contestants. Although *Drum* could have drawn on a wide range of literary achievement in selecting stories for publication, it continued to favor stories of a certain stamp. Ezekiel Mphahlele, who acted as *Drum*'s literary editor for several years but was not in full accord with *Drum*'s literary policies, complained, "I was supposed to let in the 'wet sentimental sexy stories and tough crime stories.' I tried to argue with the proprietor whenever he interviewed me that *Drum* had plunged into a reading world which hadn't developed any definite magazine taste (the non-European readership); that it should produce healthy material in an original style wherever possible and, in a sense, dictate what the public should read, without necessarily being snobbish and intellectual" (1959: 188). But *Drum* saw its mission as the satisfying of appetites rather than the shaping of tastes.

Nevertheless, *Drum* was an important pioneering publication. It was the first South African magazine of wide circulation to invite Africans to submit literary contributions in English. It discovered several talented writers and published their first stories. It solicited short stories and sketches from black writers who worked as journalists for *Drum* or for its affiliated weekly newspaper, *Golden City Post*. *Drum* awakened and kept alive a desire among blacks to write creatively in English.

Drum ceased to be an important literary magazine in 1958 when it fell under the control of a new editor[2] who was intent on making it a picture magazine. During his editorship (1958-1961) very few short stories appeared in *Drum*. In 1962 an attempt to revive *Drum*'s short story competition attracted fewer than 200 entries. Clearly, African writers were looking for publishing opportunities elsewhere.

When short stories by black South African writers stopped appearing in *Drum*, they began surfacing in two other magazines for Africans, *Zonk* and *Our Africa*. (Wilkov). Story titles such as "Runaway Bride," "Passionate Intruder," "King of Crime," "Corpse in the Life," and "Vengeance is Mine" reveal that the stories in these pop magazines did not differ much from those in *Drum*. However, the writers themselves were different. Blacks who had written for *Drum* did not write for *Drum*'s competitors.

Instead, many of them turned to the liberal, radical and Communist publications that were eager to get literary contributions from black writers, especially contributions flavored with social criticism or political protest. Collectively, these publications were as influential as *Drum* in shaping the South African short story. Certain writers with very strong political opinions—notably Alex La Guma, Richard Rive, Alfred Hutchinson, and T.H. Gwala—wrote all or most of their stories for *Fighting Talk, New Age, Africa South,* and *The New African*—publications that advocated social and political change. *Fighting Talk,* an outspoken "Monthly Journal for Democrats in Southern Africa," openly encouraged protest writing by allowing authors to use pseudonyms on stories and articles and by printing unsigned satirical sketches and excerpts from books banned in South Africa. In 1963, seventeen years after it had been established, *Fighting Talk* was banned by the government. *New Age,* a Communist weekly descended from a long line of banned Communist weeklies, sponsored short story competitions for four years (1955-1958) which attracted the kind of stories *Drum* would not dare to print. *New Age* usually awarded its prizes to stories vividly picturing situations of oppression, inequality, and injustice in South Africa. *New Age* was in its ninth year when it was banned by the government in 1962. *Africa South,* a radical quarterly designed to "assemble the different militant groups of opposition to the government in South Africa into a kind of intellectual united front" (Segal 109) and to encourage "non-white resistance to the ravages of Afrikaner rule and English-speaking exploitation" (Segal 115), published a few short stories concerned with racial conflicts before it was banned by the government in its fifth year in 1960. *Africa South* tried to resist the ban by moving to London and changing its name to *Africa South in Exile,* but after one year in exile, it expired.

As these journals disappeared, others sprang up to replace them, but they too had problems with the South African government. *The New African,* a "Radical Monthly" set up in 1962 as a forum for diverse radical views, aspired "to print verse, stories, criticism, drawings, that will find a place nowhere else in South Africa" (November 1963 issue: 1). In its first three years *The New African* published a wide variety of stories, making an effort to base its selection on literary quality rather than solely on political content. There was a healthy blend of protest literature, nonpolitical vignettes, character studies, and—most refreshing of all—humorous sketches. Unfortunately but predictably, *The New African* was continually harassed by the authorities; in March and April of 1964 its office in Cape Town was raided by the Security Police and entire issues were confiscated. In October 1964 the director of the publishing company that printed *The New African* was brought to police headquarters and charged with publishing in one of the confiscated issues an "obscene" short story by Can Themba. In court the director and the publishing company were fined a total of six hundred rands ($840). Because of continuing Security Police harassment and intimidation of its printers in South Africa, *The New African* decided to follow the example of *Africa South* by moving to London, but within a few years, it too expired.

Next there was *The Classic*, a literary quarterly started in 1963 by Nat Nakasa, an enterprising *Drum* journalist. In the first issue Nakasa wrote: "It will be the job of *The Classic* to seek African writing of merit...Particularly welcome will be the work of those writers with causes to fight for, committed men and women who look at human situations and see tragedy and love, bigotry and commonsense, for what they are...Writers must seek answers and solutions to the problems around them" (1). Even though very little protest literature appeared in the first three issues of *The Classic*, Nakasa's editorial manifesto may have worried the authorities. When Nakasa was awarded a Nieman Fellowship in 1964 to study journalism at Harvard, the South African government refused to issue him a passport. In order to take up the fellowship he had to get an exit permit, a permit allowing him to leave South Africa but not to return. With Nakasa gone, *The Classic* foundered. Even though it had financial support from the Farfield Foundation, it was silent for more than a year. The new editor, Barney Simon, struggled on and managed to bring out seven more issues over the next six years before finally letting the journal die.[3]

Aside from liberal and radical publications and pop magazines, there were few outlets for black literary expression in English. An African newspaper in Johannesburg, *Golden City Post*, occasionally published stories by black writers, but the white press and the white literary publications maintained a form of literary apartheid. Ezekiel Mphahlele remarked in his autobiography that "No South African journals circulating mainly among whites would touch any of my stories nor any others written by a non-white unless he tried to write like a European and adopted a European name" (1959: 217). A case in point was James Matthews who had written a few nonracial stories for *The Cape Argus* and *Cape Times*.

So although he lived in a multiracial society, the black writer in South Africa wrote almost exclusively for blacks. He had to try to satisfy readers with widely differing educational backgrounds, whose literary tastes, to quote Mphahlele again,

> range from Peter Cheyney and James Hadley Chase to Dickens and Shakespeare. You are dealing with masses of people who left school after Standard IV, i.e. who spent five to six years in primary school. On their own, while working, they have cultivated a reading habit. Newspapers and periodicals, detective fiction are lapped up in enormous quantities. You also have masses of people who did three years of secondary schooling and dropped out while others were climbing up. Their tastes cover detective fiction, adventure with a love interest, pure love stories and plenty of Dickens and fiction that is set in South Africa. The pyramid tapers up quite gradually into the clerical and professional occupations where interest in fiction and non-fiction evens up, and fiction reading is more wholesomely selective. (1962: 38-39)

The black writer, whether writing for *Drum* or for the liberal and radical publications, addressed readers at every level of the pyramid. He had to write about characters and situations that all his readers would understand, and he had to employ a style that all would accept. His writing thus was reduced to the lowest common denominator of his readers' experiences, interests and tastes. His audience determined what and how he wrote.

If he produced stories for magazines such as *Drum*, he wrote for an audience that wanted entertainment, excitement and diversion. Stories of love, crime, and violence were very popular, especially if they were told in a bold, authoritative manner. If he wrote for liberal or radical publications, he wrote for an audience that expected strong opinions, loud complaints and commitment to a cause. Here most of the stories realistically and sympathetically depicted the problems of blacks in a society ruled by whites. So the black writer was confronted with a choice between writing melodramatic literature for *Drum* and other pulp magazines or writing protest literature for political publications.

The worst stories in *Drum* during this era were imitations of three types of American short fiction—the true confession, the detective serial, and the underworld comedy. The true confessions, with titles such as "I Was in a Dream-land," "My Husband Was a Flirt," and "I Broke Their Hearts," were ludicrously accurate imitations. For example, in "I Was in a Dream-land" a boy and girl on a school picnic wander off to a "secluded spot" and lie down on the grass:

> We lay silent for some time. Then he rolled over and lay with his head close to mine. He was smiling. But the hungry look was still there. He kissed me. In the freedom of that quiet and deserted spot we didn't try to restrain our passions. I did not resist. He *was* the perfect lover...It was a sensation that nothing can surpass...I do not know for how long we lay there. Time glided by. We were almost late for tea. (Sefora 23)

Allied to the true confessions were the exaggerated love stories, which suffered from the same affliction—a talent for copying bad models well. These "wet sentimental sexy stories," as Mphahlele called them, were bruised with purple passages and windy with high-flown rhetoric. In one of them, Can

Themba's "Passionate Stranger," a boy falls in love with a friend's sister and declares his affection for her as soon as they are alone together:

> If my declaration sounds premature and impetuous to you, forgive me. Love is on the wing and whether I will it or no, I must join its flight...Never before has my soul echoed the resounding depths or soared the giddy heights as now...Now I know what true love can mean. Nevermore can the stars whirl and wheel the same, if you do not love me, too, Ellen. No more would the moon shed soft silver on the earth; no more would the flowers gladden the heart, the birds "untune the sky." O nevermore. I reach for your lips knowing I reach for the sun. (24)

A different American accent could be found in the language of the detective serials in *Drum*. Only a certain type of American film, American paperback, or American comic book could have inspired an African private eye to say to an African criminal, "We are going for a little ride, me and you. And don't dare call me 'bub.' I could knock your teeth down your throat for that" (Mogale, January 1953: 33). The detective serials in *Drum* were self-consciously, even boastfully derivative. One story ended with the statement, "A real made-in-America double-double-cross we made, wasn't it?" (Mogale, July 1953: 29). The private detective in these stories, patterned on an American stereotype, was strong, daring and dapper, drove a big American car, constantly outwitted his adversaries, made love to most of the women who crossed his path, and always shot to kill. Extraordinary cleverness and superhuman physical endurance got him through all his difficulties, and he brought every case to a satisfactory conclusion. Nothing about him or his adventures could be identified as authentically South African.

Underworld comedies, stories which tried to show criminals in a sympathetic or humorous light, also appeared frequently in *Drum*. The hero typically was a bumbler who had trouble earning a dishonest day's pay. The humor and idiom of Damon Runyon could be seen in several of these stories, especially in one by Bloke Modisane about a "respectable pickpocket" who was bothered by an affectionate girlfriend. "She cuddles closer and smiles in a way that interferes with my blood pressure...She throws her arms round my neck and starts kissing me like I'm distantly related to Clark Gable...Insanity is a contagious disease and listening to this woman spreading the contagion is too much for me. I take my hat and clear out" (1954: 15). Here again there was nothing South African about the language, characters or situation; everything had been imported from America.

Fortunately, several black writers who were not content to write American potboilers gave a new direction to the fiction in *Drum*. Ezekiel Mphahlele, Richard Rive and James Matthews showed that it was possible to write effective fiction about urban Africans in South Africa. Mphahlele's first story for *Drum*, a story of love and politics in a Johannesburg slum, told how a slum environment can cause human relationships to deteriorate (September 1953: 32-34). Until he left South Africa in 1957, Mphahlele continued to write stories for *Drum* about urban Africans and their problems. Matthews and Rive wrote compelling stories about *tsotsis*—the African juvenile delinquents and adult hoodlums in South African cities. Even the dialogue in these stories was unmistakably South African. Soon other African writers tried coming to grips with their environment too, and the fiction in *Drum* started to acquire a genuine South African identity.

But the change in identity was not accompanied with a change in theme or treatment. *Drum* continued to favor sensational stories of love, crime and violence. Excessive sentiment, excessive toughness, excessive bloodshed—this was the formula for the writer who wanted to sell a story to *Drum*. If he included plenty of gore and mayhem, he might win a prize in *Drum*'s short story competition. The first *Drum* competition was won by Can Themba in 1953 with "Mob Passion," a story in which a girl's lover is killed by an angry mob and the girl takes revenge into her own hands:

Quickly she picked up the axe whilst the mob was withdrawing from its prey, several of them bespattered with blood. With the axe in her hand, Mapula pressed through them until she reached the inner, sparser group. She saw Alpheus spitting upon Linga's battered body. He turned with a guttural cackle—*He-he-he! He-he-he!*—into the descending axe. It sank into his neck and down he went. She stepped on his chest and pulled out the axe. The blood gushed out all over her face and clothing. (April 1953: 48)

The violence in "Mob Passion" was surpassed in stories that appeared later. In 1955 another writer gave this account of a shebeen brawl: "A chain hook swung viciously up and down, found and lodged deep in his fat stomach, a ripping pull and his guts spilled all over the floor, his belly torn open. The scream welling up in his throat was stopped dead as a hand pike stabbed deep into his throat, a sort of coup de grace" (Hawkins 49). Fights were always described in graphic detail. A report of a fist fight in *Drum*'s prize-winning story of 1957 reached a new grotesque extreme of descriptive realism: "He made contact with a softness which was the eye of his opponent, and a jelly-like substance oozed through his broken knuckles" (Maber 55). It is evident from these examples that some of the American potboilers in *Drum* were replaced by South African potboilers.

The excesses encouraged by *Drum* could not be found in all the fiction produced by black writers in South Africa. Indeed, the most successful stories were hard-hitting realistic or naturalistic sketches of life in South Africa, stories which emphasized the plight of blacks in a society ruled by whites. Most of these appeared in the liberal and radical periodicals. The protest in such stories was often implicit; the reader, presented with a vivid picture of injustice, oppression, cruelty or poverty, was left to draw his own conclusions. In "Out of the Darkness," a story first published in *Africa South*, Alex La Guma clearly depicted African prison conditions:

> The smell of unwashed bodies and sweaty blankets was sharp, and the heat in the cell hung as thick as cotton wool...The brawl around the water buckets had subsided, since they both had been emptied. There would be no water for the rest of the night. Men sat around, hunched stark naked under the light, exploring their clothes and blankets for lice. The cracking of vermin between thumbnails sounded like snapping twigs. My own body was slippery with sweat...It was no better with the light off. The cloying heat and the stench of the latrine seemed to take advantage of the darkness. (118f)

The narrator of the story, a prisoner, describes a fellow inmate called Old Cockroach who had committed a murder when his fiancée, learning she could pass as white, had rejected him. Old Cockroach shows signs of being intelligent and well-educated, but seven years in prison have "unhinged him somewhat." Although La Guma never interrupted the narrative to shout slogans of protest, it was clear that he objected to the racial attitudes and prison conditions that destroyed his hero's life. La Guma's selection and manipulation of details conveyed his protest to the reader.

Some stories contained no protest at all. Richard Rive's "Moon Over District Six," which first appeared in *Fighting Talk*, was an impressionistic sketch of life in a Cape Town slum on New Year's Eve. Rive set the proper tone in the first paragraph: "The moon was in a recklessly gay mood and shouted, 'Happy New Year!' to the stars. The stars twinkled back respectfully, "Same to you!' The moon, a crazy whore, did a comic dance around staid spinsterly Table Mountain, and bounced dizzily across the sky. District Six hopped, skipped and jumped" (1963: 27). Rive used snapshot descriptions to capture the moods, rhythms and accents of District Six on New Year's Eve:

> "Happy New Yea', Merrim," said an early celebrator, pirouetting on the pavement in a fancy cap which read *Kiss me luvvy!*..."Your mam's tree-quarters!" said the cheeky one spitting on his dice. "Come quick, sixes my nick!"..."dere's a fight on 'e corner! Dey're

buggering up yer husband," said an urchin to a tired woman with tired breasts..."Believe in the Lord and thou shalt be saved!" foamed a street-corner Bible-thumper..."I say paaal, buy us two one an' fours," said a flashily dressed dandy in pink socks who wanted to jump the Bioscope queue. (28-30)

Explicit protest would appear to be out of place in the carefree atmosphere of District Six on New Year's Eve.

But in South African liberal and radical publications stories without protest were rare. Most often the protest was loud and undisguised. Writers boldly attacked South African laws and policies (e.g., the Group Areas Act, the pass laws, the prison labor system) or described rebellions, boycotts and police brutality. They wrote stories about racial discrimination, prejudice and snobbery, and exposed some of the painful and ironic consequences of trying to keep people of different races separated. An undercurrent of anti-white sentiment ran through a number of stories. One of Alfred Hutchinson's heroes thought to himself, "a White man would always remain a White man: he could not be otherwise. He used you and when you were torn and useless threw you away like an old shirt" (6). Alex La Guma pictured a white government official issuing passes to African women as an inhuman monster: "a row of pens and pencils form a tiny fence across his breast, as if it had been erected there to keep out all feeling of friendliness, or even minute sparks of pity or compassion. He is unemotional, expressionless, a robot, part of the vast machinery created to enslave a people" (October 1956: 8). Such blatant protest had to be carefully controlled to be effective. When message became more important than method, literary art suffered. Many of the stories in South African liberal and radical magazines were too heavy-handed to be finely drawn, too loud to be eloquent.

Black writers in South Africa in the Fifties and Sixties often found it difficult to strike a balance in their writing between the extravagant sensationalism in *Drum* and the angry protest in liberal and radical media. They either retreated to imaginary worlds or rebelled against the world in which they lived. They packed their stories full of violence, passion, sorrow, defiance, bitterness and pain. Their literature was both a reflection of and a response to their environment. It mirrored "the violence of the urban African's daily life" (Hopkinson 1959: 333), "the tempo of industrialization" (Modisane 1962: 6), the "'cold war' of colour" (Abrahams 1952), and the African's "quest for meaningful experience in the midst of a life of cultural poverty" (Nkosi 1959: 6). In such an environment, said Mphahlele, "the urges to preach, protest, hand out propaganda, to escape, sentimentalize, romanticize, to make a startling discovery in the field of race relations, to write thrillers, and other urges, all jostle for predominance in the writer" (1962: 121). His writing was conditioned by his environment.

This is not to say that such writing altogether lacked originality and accomplishment. The best writers—Alex La Guma, Richard Rive, Ezekiel Mphahlele—each developed a distinctive style and on occasion wrote very well. But it was not easy for them to write well. Even the serious artist who could resist both the financial temptation to write trash and the personal impulse to write protest might find himself unable to write with sufficient detachment. He might find it impossible to portray whites faithfully (Mphahlele 1962: 106; Abrahams 1953: 18) or to "think of human beings as human beings and not as victims of political circumstance" (Mphahlele 1959: 210). Feelings of rage, frustration or despair might spill over into his fiction, staining it with an inappropriate or irrelevant bias. He might be incapable of disengaging himself from his environment long enough to write truthfully and powerfully.

Some African writers in this predicament left South Africa to live in other parts of the world, and their writing changed. They continued to write about South Africa, but they found the time and composure to write longer works and to explore other literary forms. Peter Abrahams, the first important black South African writer-in-exile, wrote nearly a dozen novels, autobiographical works and travel books as well as a volume of short stories. Ezekiel Mphahlele wrote an autobiography, a novel and books of literary criticism and cultural commentary. Alfred Hutchinson wrote an autobiography and a play. Todd Matshikiza and Bloke Modisane also produced autobiographies, and Lewis Nkosi wrote a play, a novel and volumes of literary criticism. Much of this literature, particularly the autobiographical writing, was anti-apartheid propaganda, but it was more artful, more honest and more persuasive than the protest writing produced in South Africa. The writers, removed from their home environment, were able to sharpen their focus on it and to aim more carefully at their targets. With better control over their emotions, they had better control over their art. As Mphahlele said five years after leaving South Africa, "Excessive protest poisons one's system, and thank goodness I'm emancipated from that. The anger is there, but I can harness it" (1962: 54).

Of course, writers reacted to exile in different ways. Mphahlele felt that exile was both an emancipating and a "shattering" experience for a creative writer. It allowed him to achieve a certain degree of emotional detachment in his treatment of South Africa, but it also forced him to rely heavily on memory and to struggle to project his mind into the situation he left behind (Nkosi 1964: 8). At the same time he had to adjust to a new environment. Mphahlele found it easier to come to terms with himself in exile by writing nonfiction (February 1962: 10). His autobiography, political essays and literary criticism, as well as his later short stories, were written with a sanity, balance and strength that he was not often able to achieve as a writer in South Africa.

Bloke Modisane turned in a different direction. Before he left South Africa in 1959, he had been writing short stories for *Drum*. These were, he admitted, "innocuous short stories, escapist trash, about boxers with domestic problems, respectable pickpockets, hole-in-the-wall housebreakers, private detectives and other cardboard images of romanticism" (*Blame Me* 139). A few stories were tinged with social satire, but Modisane himself acknowledged that his writing at this time was characterized by a "broad omission of the commitment to fight against my skin, to speak out against injustice and wrong" (*Blame Me* 139). However, after arriving in London, Modisane became the angriest of the angry South African writers in exile. His autobiography, *Blame Me on History*, was a shrill scream of protest. It documented the moral and psychological disintegration of an intelligent, sensitive human being trapped in an oppressive environment. His last short stories also dealt with the consequences of possessing intelligence, sensitivity and a black skin in South Africa. In "The Situation," Modisane's best story, a university-educated African white-collar worker finds himself rejected both by the white world he wants to enter and by the black world he wants to leave; his education has made him a misfit in his environment (1963: 10-16). This kind of protest writing was a great improvement over the "escapist trash" Modisane had written for *Drum*. Like Mphahlele, Modisane had to leave South Africa before he could mature as a writer.

The few black writers in South Africa who were able to write successfully in forms other than the short story had to seek publication abroad. In 1962 a naturalistic novella by Alex La Guma, *A Walk in the Night*, was published by Mbari, a Nigerian artists and writers organization that aimed "to publish good African writing which, for commercial and 'aesthetic' reasons would not be taken by big publishing houses" (Mphahlele, December 1962: 17). A second novel by La Guma, *And a Threefold Cord*, was published in Berlin in 1964. Mbari published *Sirens, Knuckles, Boots*, a collection of poems by political activist Dennis Brutus, in 1963, and a novel by Richard Rive, *Emergency*, was published in London in 1964. Short stories by black South African writers also found a ready market abroad, many appearing in African, European and American magazines. In 1963 Richard Rive had a collection of his stories, *African Songs*, published in Germany, and he edited for an American publisher *Quartet*, an anthology of stories by four writers that was hailed by Alan Paton as "a milestone in the history of South African literature" (14). South African short-story writers and poets were always well represented in American and European anthologies of African writing.

Most of this literature published abroad was protest writing. Rive pointed out that "the only literature from the Republic which has any guarantee of selling abroad are works highly critical of the regime" (July 1963: 121). By the mid-Sixties there was no longer a market in South Africa for such literature because the government had banned virtually all the liberal and radical publications that promoted it. Protest literature was no longer tolerated in South Africa.

And protest literature published abroad had little chance of being read in South Africa. One of the provisions of South Africa's Customs Act of 1955 prohibited the importation of "indecent, objectionable or obscene" literature. Long lists of proscribed titles were printed in the *Government Gazette* with the warning that "any person who knowingly has in his possession or deals with any such publications, shall be guilty of an offence and liable on conviction to a fine of two thousand rands, or to imprisonment for a period not exceeding five years, or to both such fine and imprisonment." Nearly all the works by black writers in South Africa, as well as those by black South African writers in exile, were deemed "indecent, objectionable or obscene" and appeared in the alphabetized blacklists next to works by Erskine Caldwell, Hemingway, D.H. Lawrence, Lenin, Marx, Grace Metalious, Ellery Queen, J.D. Salinger, Mickey Spillane, Stalin, Tennessee Williams, and Richard Wright. Listed too were a wide range of periodicals, pamphlets, magazines and comic books—everything from *The Constitution of the Communist Party of China* to *Playboy* to *Hopalong Cassidy*. Sometimes a single issue of a serial publication was banned because it contained an attack on South African policies.

It was also possible for the South African government to blacklist writers so that their works could not be published at home. Under provisions of the Suppression of Communism Act of 1950 any writer suspected of being a Communist could be blacklisted. Thus, after July 30, 1962, it was unlawful for any "speech, utterance, writing or statement" by Alex La Guma or Dennis Brutus to appear in print in South Africa (Anon. 1963: 341). In 1962 La Guma was placed under continuous house arrest in Cape Town under the Detention Act; in 1964 he got into more difficulty when issues of *Fighting Talk*, a periodical banned in 1963, were found in his home. From 1963 to 1965 Dennis Brutus was in prison, first in Johannesburg, then on Robben Island.

By censoring literature from abroad, by exterminating liberal and radical publications, by blacklisting, intimidating and imprisoning writers deemed politically dangerous, the government gradually choked off protest writing in South Africa. The black writer who wanted to speak to his own people could still write fiction for *Drum*, but he could not write the kind of fiction that had appeared in *Drum* earlier. The Publications and Entertainments Act of 1963 forbade the publication in South Africa of any literature that in the opinion of the court "deals in an improper manner with murder, suicide, death, horror, cruelty, fighting, brawling, ill-treatment, lawlessness, gangsterism, robbery, crime, drunkenness, trafficking in or addiction to drugs...prostitution...passionate love scenes...night life...marital infidelity, adultery...human or social deviation or degeneracy or any other similar or related phenomenon." The Act also stated that a publication "shall be deemed to be undesirable if it...brings any section of the inhabitants of the Republic into ridicule or contempt." For a long while after 1963, *Drum*, to be on the safe side of the law, published only staff-written detective serials in which the detective's adventures took place in mythical lands and among peculiar peoples who could not be mistaken for inhabitants of South Africa.

After the draconian Publications and Entertainments Act became law, black writers in South Africa could choose between writing innocuous fantasies for a South African audience or writing protest literature for a foreign audience. Experienced writers soon started sending their manuscripts abroad. Inexperienced writers had little incentive to write. Few new black writers emerged in South Africa in the mid and late Sixties, and the promising short story movement that had gathered momentum throughout the Fifties and early Sixties was brought to an abrupt halt.

It was to take nearly a decade for black writers in South Africa to find an alternative literary form in which to express themselves. In 1971, inspired by the surprising success of a volume of verse, *Sounds of a Cowhide Drum* by Oswald Mtshali, they began turning to poetry. But that chapter in contemporary South African literary history is an entirely different story.[4]

[1] Anthony Sampson, the second editor, stayed with *Drum* for three and a half years (November 1951-March 1955) and helped to change it to a magazine designed for urban Africans. He has written a book entitled *Drum: A Venture into the New Africa* which describes the journal's first four years
[2] Tom Hopkinson has described his experiences as editor of *Drum* in *In the Fiery Continent*.
[3] *The Classic* was revived twice for brief periods by Sipho Sepamla (1975-78) and Jaki Seroke (1983-84), but it never regained its original strength.
[4] For a good selection of stories from *Drum*, see Chapman.

The Ascent and Decline of
Black Orpheus

The first issue of *Black Orpheus*, "A Journal of African and Afro-American Literature," was published in Nigeria in September 1957. Its declared purpose was "to encourage and discuss contemporary African writing" and to introduce African writers from French, Portuguese, and Spanish territories in English translation; works by West Indian and black American writers and samples of African oral literature were to be included as well. The first number, a collector's item today, contained three poems by Léopold Sédar Senghor, three poems by Gabriel Okara, a critical essay on Amos Tutuola by Gerald Moore, an essay on "The Conflict of Cultures in West African Poetry" by editor Ulli Beier, a discussion of "Ijala: the Poetry of Yoruba Hunters" by Adeboye Babalola, a conference report by co-editor Janheinz Jahn on the first World Congress of Black Writers and Artists in Paris, and reviews of Camara Laye's *The Dark Child* and Richard Wright's *Black Power*. There were photographs of hunting scenes on a carved Yoruba door and of writers and artists attending the Paris World Congress. Susanne Wenger[1] contributed an attractive silk-screen cover, a striking cover page, and lettered headings, and some of G.M. Hotop's illustrations for a German edition of Tutuola's *The Palm-Wine Drinkard* were used as vignettes. Fifty-two large pages of high-quality paper were held together by two sturdy staples. In all, it was a handsome and intelligent issue, an auspicious beginning for the publication that was to become the most important literary journal in sub-Saharan Africa.

Ulli Beier, a German living in Nigeria, was inspired to begin *Black Orpheus* after attending the first World Congress of Black

Writers and Artists organized by Présence Africaine in September 1956. There was very little writing in Nigeria or other English-speaking African countries at this time, and Beier felt that a good literary journal might help to stimulate literary activity by providing an outlet for writers and by publishing outstanding works by established black writers from other parts of Africa, the West Indies, and North and South America. The journal took its name from Jean-Paul Sartre, who coined the phrase "Black Orpheus" in his prefatory essay to the collection of French-African poetry edited by Léopold Sédar Senghor in 1948; Sartre compared the black poet's return to his native land and search within himself for his black soul, to the descent of Orpheus into Hades to reclaim Eurydice from Pluto. The journal *Black Orpheus* would help the African writer to discover himself and to rediscover his past in the great traditions of oral literature.

Beier persuaded the Nigerian Ministry of Education to publish the journal and relied heavily on material from the files of his German co-editor, Janheinz Jahn (1918-1973),[2] for the first few numbers. When Jahn resigned in 1960 after No. 6, he was replaced by Ezekiel Mphahlele and Wole Soyinka. Soyinka served until No. 14 and Mphahlele until No. 17, when Abiola Irele became co-editor. Beier himself did not leave *Black Orpheus* until 1967, and it was chiefly his energy that kept it alive and flourishing.

After the first few numbers, *Black Orpheus* was never starved for material. Beier estimates that eight out of ten manuscripts received had to be rejected. Nearly all contributions were submitted voluntarily; only a handful of critical articles and translations were solicited. While *Black Orpheus* was published by the Ministry of Education, writers were not paid, but after No. 12, when Longmans began publishing it, the Congress for Cultural Freedom provided funds for paying the contributors. Distribution of the journal was slow at first, because the Ministry of Education was inexperienced in this kind of work, but it improved when Longmans took over. Gradually, as *Black Orpheus* earned an international reputation, its circulation rose to a respectable 3,500. In Africa, writers and would-be writers read it avidly.

Black Orpheus was full of delightful surprises. Virtually every number broke new ground, ventured into undiscovered corners, revealed fresh talent. A typical issue would contain a collection of traditional poetry, fifteen poems by three or four contemporary poets, three short stories, perhaps a few folktales, two critical essays on modern literature, an essay introducing an unknown painter or sculptor, pictures and prints by at least two different artists, several photographs of traditional African art, and five book reviews. While every issue struck some kind of balance between literature and the visual and plastic arts, as well as between old and new, African and African-American, anglophone and francophone, later numbers tended to be more evenly balanced than the early ones. Africans writing in English were by then beginning to carry more weight. Keeping an alert finger on the pulse of African literary activity, *Black Orpheus* responded to currents of change by turning in new directions and pointing to new achievements. The contents of *Black Orpheus* are an index to the development of African literature in the first decade of independence.

Black Orpheus can be said to have moved through three phases. In the first, lasting roughly three years and seven issues, emphasis was placed on the literary achievements of West Indians and French West Africans, particularly on their poetry. The maiden issue contained the first English translations of Senghor, the most distinguished French-African poet. The second number featured and discussed poems by Aimé Césaire, Senghor's equal from Martinique. The third focused on Afro-Cuban poets. Of the twenty-six poets introduced in the first seven issues, eighteen were from the West Indies, two from French West Africa (Senghor and David Diop), three from America (Langston Hughes, Paul Vesey [Samuel W. Allen], Mason Jordan Mason), one from South Africa (Ezekiel Mphahlele) and two from Nigeria. Only the Nigerians, Gabriel Okara and Wole Soyinka, were new voices, both of them remarkable discoveries.

West Indians also dominated the short story, contributing six of the ten stories published in this initial phase. The best stories, two by Andrew Salkey and one by E.A. James, had an originality and boldness of style which only one other writer, Camara Laye of Guinea, was able to match. Stories by veteran writers from South Africa (Alex La Guma, Ezekiel Mphahlele) and Nigeria (Cyprian Ekwensi) were, as usual, starkly realistic.

Most of the literary criticism concentrated on established writers. Twelve of sixteen critical articles dealt exclusively with West Indian and French West African poets and novelists. The only other writers discussed at any length were Amos Tutuola, Paul Vesey [Samuel W. Allen] and Joyce Cary. Of course, there was a good reason for this imbalance. The West Indians and French West Africans had written prolifically in the fifties, and several had produced work of sufficient maturity and sophistication to interest critics. African writing in English, on the other hand, had hardly begun. Before 1960, only Tutuola and the South African Peter Abrahams seemed worthy of serious attention. Also, the purpose of *Black Orpheus* in these early years was to make known to English-speaking Africans in general and Nigerians in particular the literary achievements of their West Indian and French African cousins. During this propagandistic phase it was more important to demonstrate the excellence of the literature produced elsewhere by publishing and discussing old, established writers than to display the immaturity of African literature in English by publishing new writers who were not worth discussing. *Black Orpheus* did want to stimulate Africans to write, but it insisted that they write well. Inferior writing simply was not tolerated.

Although creative writing from English-speaking Africa seldom appeared in the early issues of *Black Orpheus*, oral traditions from these areas were often included. For example, one finds creation myths of the Yoruba and Ijaw of Nigeria and oral poetry of the Yoruba and of the Akan and Ewe of Ghana, together with informed commentary by African translators. The French-speaking territories are represented by Bayeke chants from the (Belgian) Congo, a Kono creation myth from Guinea, and a long, stately Bambara tale of courtly love from Mali. One also finds articles discussing various forms of traditional art from Dahomey, Nigeria, and the Ivory Coast. Nearly all the modern art displayed, however, is the work of European artists, usually Beier's wife Susanne Wenger, a long-time resident of Nigeria. Thus, for the older traditions of verbal and visual art *Black Orpheus* could rely on West African contributions, but for newer literary and artistic accomplishments it most often had to look elsewhere.

In the next three years, 1961-1963, the situation changed radically and *Black Orpheus* entered a new phase. West Indians and French West Africans were given far less space, Nigerians and South Africans far more. In Nigeria these were the exciting, effervescent years immediately following political independence, a time of intense literary activity. In South Africa they were the years in which African writing was being smothered under new blankets of censorship, a time when experienced writers who were not in prison or under house arrest were either fleeing the country or sending their manuscripts abroad. *Black Orpheus* provided an outlet for both the new tide in Nigeria and the old wave from South Africa.

West Indian and francophone African writers still made substantial contributions, but they no longer dominated the journal. Their gradual displacement by Africans writing in English can be observed in Nos. 8-13, but most dramatically in No. 12 which contains no West Indian or French-African poems, stories, oral traditions, art or literary criticism. All the literary contributions in this number were prize-winning entries in a writing competition organized by Mbari in 1962, and all were by South Africans or anglophone West Africans. *Black Orpheus* was consequently busy reaping the new harvest.

The poetry in these issues was exciting. The number of Nigerian poets had suddenly grown; John Pepper Clark made his debut in No. 10, Christopher Okigbo in No. 11, Michael Echeruo in No. 12, and Gabriel Okara and Wole Soyinka, who had been introduced earlier, were seen again. Lenrie Peters of the Gambia, George Awoonor-Williams (now Kofi Awoonor) of Ghana, and Dennis Brutus and Arthur Nortje of South Africa were also discovered during this period. From the French territories there were further translations of Senghor and Césaire, as well as pioneer translations of Tchicaya U Tam'si of the (French) Congo, and of Flavien Ranaivo and Jean-Joseph Rabéarivelo of Madagascar, but the balance had obviously shifted. Africans writing in English now supplied about half of the poetry published in *Black Orpheus*.

They also supplied more than half the fiction. Practiced South African short-story writers such as Alex La Guma, Alf Wannenburgh, Bloke Modisane, and Arthur Maimane wrote powerful protest literature, while the Nigerians Nkem Nwankwo, Gabriel Okara, Horatio Edward Babatunde Jones, and the Ghanaian Christina [Ama Ata] Aidoo experimented with form and technique. Two new writers from Sierra Leone, Gaston Bart-Williams and Christina Attarrah, offered humorous stories, and a Kenyan, Grace Ogot, told a modern East African fairy tale. Though the West Indians, francophone Africans and African Americans were now outnumbered, they continued to make their presence felt by contributing some of the most daringly original and accomplished fiction in *Black Orpheus*.

While all this new literary activity was going on, the critics were silent. Only three critical articles appeared, one on Langston Hughes, the other two introducing Flavien Ranaivo and Tchicaya U Tam'si. The West Indians and francophone Africans who had attracted a great deal of attention in the first numbers of *Black Orpheus* were no longer mentioned; the new writers springing up in every issue were perhaps too new and too little published to be intelligently discussed. For the critics it was a time of watching and waiting, a time for writing book reviews rather than lengthy articles. During this period, many more reviews in *Black Orpheus* were devoted to African novels, plays and poetry in English.

Black Orpheus changed in other ways, too. All the traditional literature published—Malozi and Wapangwa creation myths, Luo songs, Swahili poetry—now came from East and Central rather than West Africa, and the art work displayed and discussed was more frequently African than European. *Black Orpheus* introduced such gifted artists as Demas Nwoko of Nigeria, Vincent Akweti Kofi of Ghana, Ibrahim Salahi of the Sudan, and Valente Goenha Malangatana of Mozambique, and occasionally reviewed exhibitions of their work. It also publicized the work of several talented artists from Brazil, Germany and the United States. A restless explorer, *Black Orpheus* was constantly seeking new horizons.

In its next four years, *Black Orpheus* continued to discover exciting young writers and artists and also drew heavily on those it had introduced earlier. Africans writing in English remained prominent but not as dominant as in the preceding phase. *Black Orpheus* was now more cosmopolitan, better balanced, and its contributions more accomplished, more assured. Having passed through a West Indian infancy and a West African adolescence, it had now achieved full maturity, a rich, solid and complex ripeness.

Among the poets who made their first appearance in *Black Orpheus* during this period were Agostinho Neto of Angola, Mbella Sonne Dipoko of the Cameroons, David Rubadiri of Malawi, Cliff Lashley of Jamaica, K.N. Darwulla of India, Joseph Miezan Bognini of the Ivory Coast, LeRoi Jones, A.B. Spellman, and Paul Theroux of the United States, and Okogbule Wonodi, Pol N. Ndu, Romanus Egudu, Clem. Abiaziem Okafor and Bona Onyejeli of Nigeria. The Nigerians, interestingly enough, were all students or graduates of the University of Nigeria at Nsukka, which is surprising since nearly all the Nigerian poets published in earlier issues of *Black Orpheus* had been graduates of Ibadan University. This suggests that there were two distinct schools of poetry growing up in Nigeria, the older one with its roots at Ibadan, the younger emanating from Nsukka.

The twenty-five writers who published fiction in the later numbers of *Black Orpheus* hailed from sixteen different countries and wrote in at least as many different styles. Camara Laye of Guinea contributed a hauntingly symbolic fantasy, Sylvain Bemba of the Congo a story of an African student in Paris going mad, Mongo Beti of the Cameroons a hilarious account of a seduction, Chinua Achebe of Nigeria a political satire, Jan Carew of Guiana an exquisite fable, Henri Krea of Algeria a war story, Olympe Bhêly-Quénum of Dahomey a tale of a tough African Robin Hood, D.O. Fagunwa of Nigeria a description of a hunter's wrestling match with a sixteen-eyed monster. These remarkably heterogeneous stories had one thing in common: every one was very well written.

The literary critics now focused much of their attention on African writing in English, especially works from Nigeria. The achievements of Wole Soyinka, John Pepper Clark, Chinua Achebe and D.O. Fagunwa were carefully assessed in individual essays, and the salient features of Nigerian market chapbooks were described in an amusing article. There were surveys of South African fiction, anglophone African poetry and Southern Bantu literature, as well as thematic articles on "African Literature and the African Personality," "Africa in West Indian Literature," and "The Negro Poet and His Landscape." Other essays dealt with Claude McKay and Cliff Lashley of Jamaica, Agostinho Neto of Angola, two black Latin poets, and three African autobiographies written in the eighteenth century. During this period African writing in English continued to dominate the book review section.

Except for a few South African and Egyptian poems, an Amharic love song, some Brazilian lorry inscriptions, and scattered folktales, the traditional literature in the last numbers of *Black Orpheus* was entirely West African and primarily Nigerian. Since the journal was published in the heart of Yorubaland, it is not surprising that much of the Nigerian material—sacred chants, divination verses, funeral songs, riddles, folktales—was Yoruba. Lengthy essays on Hausa and Igbo poetry, however, helped to offset this imbalance.

The art work too was now predominantly Nigerian, nearly all of it by contemporary artists working in different media. There were paintings by Colette Omogbai and Demas Nwoko, lino cuts by Jacob Afolabi and Rufus Ogundele, a silk-screened cover design by Adebisi Fabunmi, vignettes by Muraina Oyelami, sculpture by Adebisi Akanji, metal work by Asiru and terrra-cotta reliefs by O. Idah. There were illustrated articles on the etchings of Twins Seven Seven and the naive sign paintings of untrained artists in Nigerian cities. From non-Nigerian artists there were vignettes by Hezbon Owiti of Kenya and eight-year-old Pedro Guedes of Mozambique, calligraphy by Shibrain of the Sudan, paintings by A. Chandra, and cover designs and vignettes by Susanne Wenger and Georgina Beier. The only traditional art objects pictured were some terrra-cotta toys made by the Falashas of Ethiopia. In art as in literature, *Black Orpheus* had come a long way in ten short years.

Although it may never be possible to measure precisely the amount of influence that *Black Orpheus* had on the development of African literature during its first decade, there is evidence to suggest that it was a powerful source of stimulation and inspiration for a number of African authors, particularly in Nigeria. Besides encouraging writers by publishing their first works, *Black Orpheus* showed them what their contemporaries at home and abroad were writing. Several writers appear to have made use of ideas gleaned from its pages. Under the Yoruba pseudonym of Obotunde Ijimere,[3] Ulli Beier based his play *Woyengi* on an Ijaw folktale told by Gabriel Okara in *Black Orpheus*, No. 2. Beier's play *The Imprisonment of Obatala* and J.P. Clark's poem of the same title may have been inspired by Susanne Wenger's handling of a Yoruba myth on her batiks, one of which was reproduced and described in No. 7. Christopher Okigbo's poem "Lament of the Lavender Mist" in No. 11 with its recurring image of "black dolls" appears to owe something to Leon Damas's poem "Black Dolls" in No. 2. Also, several novelists used the pages of *Black Orpheus* to try out new ideas which were later developed into full-length works. A version of the first chapter of Gabriel Okara's experimental novel, *The Voice* (1964), was published in No. 10. Details from Chinua Achebe's story "The Voter" in No. 17 are echoed in his novel, *A Man of the People* (1966). Amos Tutuola's story "Ajaiyi and the Witchdoctor" in No. 9 may have been the starting point for his longest work of fiction, *Ajaiyi and His Inherited Poverty* (1967). These are only the most obvious examples. It would be very hard to find an early Nigerian writer who could claim to have completely escaped the influence of *Black Orpheus*. They all read it and many wrote for it.

While it made its greatest impact in Nigeria, *Black Orpheus* also exercised an influence abroad. It continued to draw contributions from the entire black world, publishing in ten years works by 224 writers and artists from twenty-six African nations, fourteen West Indian and Latin American states, England, Germany, Sweden, India, Iran, Indonesia and the United States. More important, it was read by a discriminating international audience quick to recognize and applaud original talent. *Black Orpheus* thus served as a first-class publicity agent and promoter for new African and African-American writers and artists, helping to make them known to the outside world.

Black Orpheus owes its initial reputation and longevity to the industry, intelligence and skill of its editor, Ulli Beier. He was its architect, co-ordinating engineer, mason, day laborer, and work-horse; in ten years, sometimes under pseudonyms such as Sangodare Akanji and Omidiji Aragbabalu, he wrote twenty-two articles, fifty reviews, and forty translations for *Black Orpheus*, many of them breaking new ground in unexplored regions of the arts. The first decade of *Black Orpheus* stands as a landmark in African literary history, a monument to black creativity. It is also a monument to Ulli Beier, the man who made it what it was.

When Beier left Nigeria for Papua New Guinea in 1967, many of its devoted readers feared that *Black Orpheus* would perish. The country was becoming embroiled in a civil war, many talented Igbo writers had fled to secessionist Biafra, and the literary movement which *Black Orpheus* had helped to set in motion looked as if it was about to come to an abrupt halt. There was talk that the magazine would continue under new editorship, but as the war gathered momentum, this idea was dismissed, even by the most sanguine observers, as mere talk. *Black Orpheus* seemed doomed.

There were writers and artists in Nigeria, however, who were determined to keep it alive. In 1968 playwright John Pepper Clark and critic Abiola Irele teamed up to edit the first issue of the "new" *Black Orpheus* (Vol. 2, No. 1) and announced that two more issues, one devoted to traditional African literatures and another to politics and the arts in Africa, would appear within a year. It actually took a bit longer than twelve months for these issues to materialize, but over the next five years or so, Clark and Irele managed to bring out an average of one issue per year, enabling the journal to survive the civil war and its aftermath.

The new *Black Orpheus* looked very much like the old. It had the same size, same format, same kind of striking silk-screen cover, many of the same contributors, roughly the same price, and even some of the same typographical errors. There was a reassuring air of constancy and familiarity about it which conveyed the impression that it would continue to do exactly the kind of work it had done so well in the past. This was a misleading surface impression, however, for there were also clear signs that *Black Orpheus* had changed, that it would henceforth move quite deliberately in a rather different direction.

The first evidence of a break with the past could be found in its new subtitle. Under Beier, *Black Orpheus* was called "A Journal of African and Afro-American Literature," and literary and artistic contributions were solicited from all parts of the black world. West Indians and French West Africans tended to dominate the early issues, with English-speaking West Africans, particularly Nigerians, coming to the fore in the early and mid-sixties. Though the journal became somewhat less cosmopolitan in its later issues, it was never parochial. Guineans stood cheek by jowl with Guianans or Ghanaians or Guadeloupeans or even Germans; articles on Nigerian pop art were balanced by studies of Cuban rumba rhythms, Arabic calligraphy, or Swahili poetry; the literary pages occasionally admitted an odd Swede, Persian, East Indian, or American Peace Corps volunteer. Each issue was an international potpourri.

But under Clark and Irele, *Black Orpheus* appeared to have a much narrower geographical range. The first issue in the new series was subtitled "A Journal of the Arts from Africa," the second "A Journal of the Arts in Africa." Virtually all the contributors were Nigerians, Ghanaians, or white expatriates working in these two countries, and their contributions dealt almost exclusively with West African literature, art, music or dance. Such a close regional focus was perhaps unavoidable in the circumstances. It is difficult enough to resurrect a half-dead literary review in times of peace and tranquillity. To do so during a civil war, with one editor out of the country (Irele was in Ghana), required extra resourcefulness and perseverance. So it was not surprising that Clark and Irele had to rely primarily on material they could scare up from their friends and colleagues. To have waited for promised manuscripts to arrive from other parts of Africa would have delayed publication indefinitely. Of course, since they did solicit a number of contributions from writers outside West Africa, some of the later issues of the new *Black Orpheus* had a slightly wider scope, but not one ranged quite as freely from continent to continent in search of new black talent as had most of the issues of its predecessor.

Nevertheless, the reincarnated *Black Orpheus*, despite its new geographical isolationism, managed to remain sufficiently diversified in content. The first issue contained poetry by Ken Saro-Wiwa, Aig Higo, Bruce King (an American), and the late Christopher Okigbo; an anonymous short story on a political theme; a definition of "The Language of African Music" by composer Akin Euba; an essay by J.P. Clark on the issue of the English language in African literature; a description by Jamaican Lindsay Barrett of stage designer Demas Nwoko's studio in

Ibadan; reviews of a Yoruba novel, a book of Yoruba proverbs, and Ugandan poet Okot p'Bitek's *Song of Lawino*; and art work by Bruce Onobrakpeya. The second issue, a special number devoted to traditional African literatures, featured transcriptions and translations of Yoruba Ifa divination verses, an Idoma ancestral mask chant, and the prologue to an Ijaw saga; there was also a brief account of the Ghana Dance Ensemble by Oyin Ogunba, a long essay on "The Poetry of Akan Drums" by the distinguished ethnomusicologist from Ghana, J.H. Kwabena Nketia, some poems by Samson Amali, art work by Demas Nwoko, and reviews of Edward Brathwaite's long poem *Rights of Passage* and S.A. Konadu's novel *A Woman in Her Prime*. Several of these contributions merit further comment.

Certainly the most exciting reading in the first issue was Christopher Okigbo's poetry. These were probably Okigbo's last works, for he was killed early in the war while serving as a major in the Biafran army. Most of the poems are dated, so one can see they were written between December 1965 and May 1966, the period during which Nigeria experienced its first military coup, then a counter-coup followed by massacres of Igbos in the North. Okigbo, an Igbo, was reacting to these events in his poems, which are collectively called "Path of Thunder." An obituary facing the first poem in the group declares that "his 'chant' forms a personal, prophetic record of the torment and trauma of a nation in tragic grip of self-recognition," and the editors took the liberty of placing an additional title, "Poems Prophesying War," above "Path of Thunder." The poems do indeed seem prophetic for they are filled with fearful images of iron, violence, and gathering storms. Later poems, which describe what happens after the thunder has broken, are saturated with visions of the machinery of war—howitzers, detonators, bayonets, cannons, "the iron dance of mortars," etc.; these were written at least a year before the civil war broke out.

But Okigbo's poetry is never just a metaphorical prophecy of armed conflict. Each poem has a number of interrelated meanings, for Okigbo is one of the few African poets who can move along several planes of significance simultaneously. Moreover, he is an exceedingly musical lyricist with an extraordinarily subtle control over rhythm and sound. "Path of Thunder" reveals that he was still growing as an artist, still exploring fresh territory—this time in the murkiest corners of the human spirit. It is a tragedy that he was lost to African literature during the cataclysm he foresaw.

The other highlight of the maiden issue was Clark's essay, "The Legacy of Caliban." Borrowing from Shakespeare's *Tempest* the image of Prospero and Caliban in conflict, which has been used by political scientists, historians, and psychologists as a paradigm of the colonial situation, Clark argues that the African writer who, like Caliban, expresses himself in his foreign master's tongue, must strive to remain true to himself and his own vernacular idiom while doing so. He must create an authentic indigenous style in an alien language. "The African writer thus occupies a position not unlike that of an ambidextrous man, a man placed in the unique and advantageous position of being able to draw strength from two separate equal sources. His is a gift of tongues."

An opportunity to study how effectively Clark himself utilized this gift was provided in the next issue of *Black Orpheus*, which carried a partial translation of the seven-night saga upon which Clark had based his English play *Ozidi*(1966). Only the beginning of the prologue to the first night of the saga was reproduced, but the events in this portion of the epic narrative corresponded quite closely to those dramatized by Clark in the first act of *Ozidi*. A great warrior is killed by conspirators, and his son, who will later avenge his death, is born. Clark embroiders not only the action but the language of the original to create a work which has an integrity of its own yet clearly owes its inspiration to native sources. Such passages prove that Clark has not just a "gift of tongues" but a gift for theater.

Another highlight of the second issue was Nketia's lucid discussion of the types of poetry produced in Akan society on talking drums. Nketia, an expert on the subject, gives detailed descriptions of the drums and drummers as well as of the drumming, and the reader cannot help but be impressed by the musical sophistication and rigorous training required of those who aspire to become "custodians of drum poetry." Drumming is a high art in Africa, but among the Akan (and presumably many other West African peoples) it is also something of a science. Nketia's essay, a masterful ethnomusicological study, takes us into an exciting musical universe.

Such interesting contributions made one willing to forgive the new *Black Orpheus* for its erratic publishing schedule, its myopically regional focus on Nigeria and Ghana, and some of its genuinely bad poetry. It was clear that there was still some life left in this revitalized organ.

By the time the third issue appeared, Okigbo was dead and the war had almost run its course. Three laments for Okigbo by Igbo, Yoruba and British poets opened the issue, followed by essays and poems gathered around the topic "Literature and Politics in English-speaking Africa." Despite its emphasis on anglophone areas, this was a better balanced issue than the two preceding; it had articles by South Africa's Ezekiel Mphahlele and East Africa's Ali Mazrui and Okot p'Bitek as well as Gerald Moore's critical study of "Poetry and the Nigerian Crisis," and clusters of poems by Nigerian, American and Caribbean authors, including the early black nationalist Marcus Garvey. Indeed, it began to look as if *Black Orpheus* was returning to its earlier international orientation.

But the next issue (Vol. 2, No. 4) narrowed the journal's range of focus once again, this time limiting it almost exclusively to studies of Nigerian art and architecture. A few poems by Congolese and Ghanaian bards and a routine survey article on "Modern Drama in West Africa" by Oyin Ogunba did little to correct the imbalance. *Black Orpheus* now seemed to be sliding back into parochialism.

However, it achieved a new height of diversity again in Vol. 2, Nos. 5-6, a double issue devoted primarily to the novel in Africa. Essays by scholars from Africa, Europe and the United

States on such writers as Camara Laye, Ferdinand Oyono, Peter Abrahams, Ignatius Sancho, Ottobah Cugoano, Chinua Achebe, Gabriel Okara and Wole Soyinka took up more than half the space, and an assortment of poetry, fiction, reviews and even pedagogical and bibliographical contributions rounded out the rest of the issue, giving it that old international flavor once again.

But the editors could not sustain this outward momentum. The next issue was given over almost entirely to things Nigerian. The only significant "foreign" element was a group of seven superb "Harmattan Poems" by the talented West Indian poet Edward Brathwaite. As before, the pendulum had swung back in an easy homeward direction.

Between 1972 and 1974 *Black Orpheus* ceased publication and appeared moribund. Abiola Irele withdrew from the editorial board and launched a new journal, *The Benin Review*, which did not survive beyond its first two issues. J.P. Clark, however, re-resurrected *Black Orpheus* in mid-1974, publishing it from the University of Lagos, where he was Chairman of the English Department. It was billed as a "bi-annual, devoted to the arts of Africa and related lands," and it looked very much like its predecessors. The first issue (Vol. 3, No. 1) was dominated by Nigerian contributors but included some interesting war poems by Gabriel Okara, a piece on African music by Akin Euba, a few strident poems by African-American Jayne Cortez, and a play prepared by Martin Banham for a drama workshop at the University of Sierra Leone. In all, it was a respectable start for a second rebirth of the journal.

The next number did not appear for more than a year, eventually being published as a double issue (Vol. 3, Nos. 2-3). In an apology to subscribers, the editor explained that *Black Orpheus* "has been suffering from the usual publication delays that at present plague most journals in the country," but he hoped to "regularize" production by the end of 1976. The issue was almost evenly split between Nigerian and African-American contributors, with Dennis Brutus being arbitrarily placed among the Americans in the table of contents. The most significant pieces were poems by Sonia Sanchez and Robert Hayden, an excerpt from a war novel by Flora Nwapa, and a pioneering study by J.P. Clark's wife Ebun of the content and form of Hubert Ogunde's popular theatrical works in Yoruba.

But this was the most cosmopolitan issue that *Black Orpheus* was to produce in its third revived phase. Vol. 3, No. 4, edited by Nnabuenyi Ugonna, was another nearly all-Nigerian affair, the major ingredients being a set of oral poems translated from various Nigerian languages, an excerpt from another unpublished novel by Flora Nwapa, a solid study of "Rhetoric in Modern Nigerian Literature" by Robert Wren, and a rather strange critical essay entitled "Literature and the Cosmic Schizophrenic Tendencies of Man" by Sulayman S. Nyang. Even the two foreign contributors to this issue—the American Wren and the Ugandan Erisa Kironde—were living and working in Nigeria. The journal had become an exclusively domestic product.

Five years were to pass before another issue of *Black Orpheus* materialized. Editor Ugonna explained in a prefatory note to Vol. 4, No. 1 (1981) that "*Black Orpheus* has passed through a difficult period over the past two [sic] years. We are glad to announce that the problems have been overcome. With this special number, we are re-launching the journal on its distinguished course. *Black Orpheus* will retain its character of being a venue for publishing creative and critical works on the black world." However, the contents of the new number belied this claim, for they consisted entirely of a selection of papers presented at a conference held in Lagos three years earlier on "The Inter-relationship of the Arts in Nigeria." Again all the contributors were Nigerians or expatriates living in Nigeria. The rest of the black world was not represented. Putting in print a collection of old academic papers may have been a convenient way to jump-start a stalled vehicle, but it gave the impression that *Black Orpheus* was slipping backward toward a tired parochialism rather than moving forward to a re-energized cosmopolitanism.

The next two issues, edited now by Theo Vincent, helped to steer the journal back to its original direction. Vol. 4, No. 2 (1982) carried a short story by a Zimbabwean writer, Chinjara Hopewell Seyaseya; two critical articles on African-American literature by African-American scholars Marlene Mosher and Darwin T. Turner; an essay on the Togolese popular novelist Felix Couchoro by Sabit Adeyboyega Salami, a Nigerian scholar; reviews of a critical study of Camara Laye and of a wide-ranging survey of African literature edited by Ulli Beier; and poems by African-American and Nigerian poets. Vol. 5, No. 1 (1983) extended the journal's international range by publishing poetry by Swaebou Conateh of the Gambia, Kofi Anyidoho of Ghana, Syl Cheyney-Coker of Sierra Leone, and Gabriel Okara of Nigeria; essays on Léopold Senghor and on Yoruba oral poetry for children; and a review of a volume of verse by Reynold S. Francis of Antigua. It looked as if *Black Orpheus* was beginning to resume its earlier Pan-African focus.

But in the years that followed the resurgent momentum generated during this brief interlude could not be sustained, and *Black Orpheus* gave signs not just of slowing down but of stopping altogether. Since 1983 only three slim issues have appeared, the latest—Vol. 6, No. 2 (1993)—a surprise after a seven-year hiatus. And these issues have relied all too heavily on Nigerian contributions. The occasional poem by a Sierra Leonean, short story by a Guianan and critical essay by a Ghanaian have not been enough to redeem the claim, still asserted on the title page of each issue, that *Black Orpheus* remained "A Journal of the Arts in Africa."

Even if it re-emerges phoenix-like from its ashes once again, it is unlikely that *Black Orpheus* will regain the influence it had in its first decade of existence. Indeed, one must admit that the journal revived and re-revived so many times since Ulli Beier left it nearly thirty years ago has been only a shadow of its former self. Its irregularity of publication and inability to attract a steady flow of manuscripts from outside Nigeria combined to vitiate its impact on the African literary scene. Also, a very poor distribution system made *Black Orpheus* virtually impossible to obtain anywhere but in Lagos so that even its most enthusiastic fans abroad were unable to read it anymore. As a relic of the past or as a literary magazine of modest regional circulation, it may be able to survive a little longer on the strength of its name alone, but as an important cultural outlet, as a major catalyst of creative expression in the black world, *Black Orpheus* died a long time ago.[4]

[1] On this artist's contribution to Nigerian culture, see Beier 1975.

[2] For information on Jahn and his works, see the obituary and bibliography prepared by Schild.

[3] Jahn was the first to reveal that this was one of Beier's pseudonyms; see Jahn, et al 149-151. For further details, see Owomoyela 1979.

[4] For a more detailed account of the history of *Black Orpheus* up to 1984, see Benson.

African Little Magazines

Little magazines have played a big role in the development of anglophone African writing. Indeed, virtually all the major authors in English-speaking Africa today got their start in local periodicals of very limited circulation. They wrote for their peers rather than for international consumption.

Usually the process began in high school, where they contributed to the school annual, to house and club news sheets, and to whatever other campus publications needed their words to fill up vacant space. When these literary apprentices moved on to the university, they found greater opportunities for extracurricular creativity in specialized serials that catered to the undergraduate community. Sometimes they would enthusiastically appropriate these organs, serving as editors, managers, columnists or freelance stringers who collectively or individually carried the full burden of producing issues at fairly regular intervals over a nine-month term. In the early years of University College Ibadan, for instance, Chinua Achebe took on the responsibility of editing the *University Herald*, a well-established Students' Union journal; Wole Soyinka ran *The Eagle*, a satirical broadsheet associated with the Progressive Party, a student political organization that regularly lost campus elections; and J.P. Clark energetically edited not only an influential undergraduate poetry magazine (*The Horn*) and a Students' Union annual (*Beacon*) but also a new Ijaw cultural journal (*Aro*) that, rather like Mammy Water, disappeared immediately after its tantalizing maiden appearance. At Makerere University College in Uganda the same pattern repeated itself: James Ngugi (now world-famous as Ngugi wa Thiong'o), Peter Nazareth and John Nagenda were among the first editors of *Penpoint*, a literary magazine published by the English Department that provided one of the earliest outlets for East African efforts at belletristic self-expression.

After their university years these young writers who had kept campus media alive tended to remain active in publications work as editors, contributors or spirited boosters. Soyinka and Clark served as editors of *Black Orpheus* for a number of years. Soyinka also edited *Transition* for a brief spell in the mid-1970s and threw his weight behind a new journalistic venture in Nigeria in the mid-1980s by writing an occasional editorial column for a weekly news magazine called *The African Guardian*. After the Nigerian civil war Achebe founded and edited *Nsukkascope* at the University of Nigeria and simultaneously launched *Okike*, possibly Africa's finest literary journal. Ngugi edited *Zuka* in the late 1960s, and he, Nazareth and Nagenda wrote frequently for *Transition* and other East African cultural magazines. Out of this kind of ardent promotional activity these pioneers helped to create and sustain a climate of creativity in tropical Africa that rapidly produced an astonishingly rich literary harvest. Indeed, it would be no exaggeration to say that little magazines were the primary fertilizing agents underlying Africa's modern literary flowering. Without them it is unlikely that the first fruits would have ripened so suddenly and so splendidly.

But where are these little magazines today? The original *Transition* died two decades ago, having proved itself incapable of being fully reborn as *Ch'indaba*; it was restarted in the United States in 1991 by Henry Louis Gates, Jr., with Soyinka listed on the masthead as Chairman of the Editorial Board, no doubt an honorific title. *Black Orpheus* went into a long period of quiescence punctuated by brief flickers of life, but it appears to be irrevocably moribund today. *Zuka* and *Nsukkascope* perished after they had served their transitory purposes, and the campus publications faded away into oblivion. *Okike*'s publishing rhythm has been slowed and permanently set off cycle so it is now more than five years out of sync, if indeed it is still alive. Does this high mortality rate among Africa's most vital organs signal the end to an era of rapid growth? Has the fertilizer vanished, robbing the continent of its fecundity and promise? Are we headed toward another long season of aridity, toward gradual reencroachment of a giant desert? To put it more plainly, are we now witnessing signs of the slow strangulation and imminent death of African literature?

Certainly not! There is plenty of evidence of other sorts to show that the creative spirit not only is alive and well in most corners of the continent but also in certain places is remarkably robust and virile. Little magazines are only one index of the health of a literate society, and it is precisely because they are "little" and thus by their very nature vulnerable to obliteration by bigger forces in the public arena that they come and go with such frequency. Kole Omotoso once remarked on what he called the "abiku complex" in African journal publishing, comparing the evanescent nature of many of these publications to that of spirit children who live awhile, then die and get reborn, usually to the same cursed mother. It's an apt comparison, but one should remember that this kind of curse can also be a blessing, for it forces the parents to be endlessly creative in reasserting the primacy of life. If one child dies, another must be conceived to take its place. Maintaining the cycle of creativity may be more important than extending the existence of each individual creation. This line of reasoning is analogous to the argument that the termite was crucial to the development of strong traditions of African wood sculpture, for by eating away the old masterpieces, it forced artists to carve excellence anew—in other words, to maintain the acuity of their creative skills through constant exercise. The same could be said of little magazines: what is most significant about these short-lived vehicles is not their hasty demise but rather their regular resurrection, their continuity in new guises.

Frederick Crews, writing about the role of such ephemeral media in American cultural life, states that

"Little magazines" are, for the most part, the mayflies of the literary world. Launched on implausibly idealistic manifestoes, briefly sustained by charity and overwork, and imperiled by an ever-worsening ratio of creditors to subscribers, they soon complete their scarcely noticed flights and sink away, to be replaced by swarms of others. Ephemerality is the little magazine's generic fate; by promptly dying it gives proof that it remained loyal to its first program. Conversely, when such a journal survives for decades and effects a change in the whole temper of cultural debate, we may be sure that a metamorphosis has occurred. In outward respects—format, financing, even the number of paying readers—the magazine may still be technically "little," but its editors will have shown a quite untypical gift for retreating from untenable positions. (195-196)

Part of this statement may not be entirely relevant here, for there are hardly any African little magazines except *Black Orpheus* and *Transition* that could be said to have grown truly "big," and both of these proved in the end to be just as ephemeral as the others, though perhaps less for ideological reasons than for political or economic ones.[1] But Crews reminds us of the inherent instability of creative media anywhere in a changing world. His position is not unlike that of the Onitsha pamphleteer who warns us that "NO CONDITION IS PERMANENT."

Where then is it possible to find traces of continuity amidst the churning flux that overwhelms every cultural environment, including that in which African little magazines emerge? One such place is the university campus, that hothouse of incipient intellectualism where tiny seeds of new ideas get planted, germinate, take root and grow. Most African universities, in seeking to encourage their undergraduates to think creatively, have provided outlets for self-expression that are relatively free from institutional administrative control. Where this is not the case, the students themselves, aided by sympathetic members of the faculty, sometimes have set up their own channels of unfettered communication. The printed products produced in this ambiance of literary liberty range from handbills and flimsy news sheets to cyclostyled magazines and typeset journals. One characteristic unites them all: they are campus media meant to give voice to the relatively voiceless, to those young men and women who seldom or never have been heard from before. This is an arena in which quiet undergraduates can shed their inhibitions and lose their verbal virginity in some safety among their own agemates. The University of Ibadan's *Idoto* (a successor to *The Horn*), the University of Nigeria's *Omabe* (a long-standing sequel to *Fresh Buds*, a poetry magazine to which Okigbo himself once contributed), the University of Ife's *Ijala* (which followed earlier Writers Workshop publications such as *Sokoti* and *Ife Writing*), Makerere University's *Makerere Beat* (which emerged as a descendant of *Penpoint* during the Amin years), the University of Nairobi's *Mwangaza wa Fasihi* (the mild-mannered heir-apparent to a more political Literature Students Association journal called *Mzalendo*, which surfaced after Ngugi's detention), and totally new ventures such as the University of Port Harcourt's *Ofirima*, the University of Zimbabwe's *The Student's Eye*, the University of Botswana's *The Artist's Pot* and the University of Zululand's *Celebration* are all examples of this kind of self-renewing student-centered publishing enterprise on African university campuses. This is the bottom rung on the ladder of literary self-advancement, and even if it disappears for a time, eventually it will reestablish itself under a new banner as a necessary first step in the struggle for articulate identity. As long as there are undergraduates, there will always be undergraduate little magazines.

Another type of academic publication several rungs higher is the journal devoted to literary or cultural commentary. Here is where faculty and advanced postgraduate students can try our their ideas and occasionally engage in polite polemics. Given the relative scarcity of independent and truly international professional journals of literary scholarship and criticism in most African countries (*African Literature Today* edited at the University of Sierra Leone may be the only one in the whole of anglophone black Africa, and it now comes out less than once a year), these in-house organs may provide the only local opportunities for university literary scholars to display their professional expertise. There may be no other way for them to reach colleagues directly through the printed word, and since their future prospects, including their eligibility for promotion, may depend on the opinions such colleagues form of them and their work, it behooves them to contribute regularly to whatever domestic media are available. So these journals, being more intimately connected with matters of academic life and death, tend to be sturdier and wordier than the student literary magazines. They too seem to be a permanent fixture in the architecture of any university.

There is a danger, of course, that such inbred publications, in the absence of wider communicative intercourse, will grow, like old world royal families, incestuous, dull and idiotic. But alert editors may try to guard against such tendencies by including from time to time seminal contributions from outside the compound walls. A visiting professor might be asked to contribute something, or manuscripts might be solicited from selected colleagues some distance away. In large countries— Nigeria, for example, with more than twenty universities to draw from—all that is needed is a brief announcement that a new journal welcomes unsolicited manuscripts, and a small avalanche of papers soon follows. But in smaller countries, especially those having but a single national university, it may be more difficult and less desirable to achieve wide geographical representation among contributors. For quite understandable reasons, a national university may prefer to offer its only public platform to its own faculty and faculty-in-training. All else being equal, parity begins at home.

Examples of academic journals that specialize in literary or cultural commentary are not uncommon in Africa today, but specimen copies sometimes can be exceedingly hard to find. Inadequate off-campus distribution has made many of these highbrow little magazines even littler than they need to be. *Fourah Bay Studies in Language and Literature, Calabar Studies in Modern*

Languages, Lagos Review of English Studies, Cameroon Studies in English and French, NJALA: New Approaches to Language Arts, Ibadan Journal of Humanistic Studies, Nigerian Journal of the Humanities, Ife Studies in African Literature and the Arts, Ife Monographs on Literature and Criticism, Nsukka Studies in African Literature, Working Papers in African Literature, Work in Progress, Saiwa, Afa, Nkà, Kiabàrà, Ganga, Gwani, Hekima, Marang, Pula, Ngoma, Ngam, Mould, New Horizons, Nigerian Theatre Journal, African Theatre Review, and *Journal of the Performing Arts* would no doubt be classified as rare and exotic periodicals by university librarians the world over, and that world includes all of Africa. Back numbers of these serials are even more difficult to locate and have been known to elude intrepid researchers who have trekked to libraries on the very campuses where they were issued. In the marketplace of ideas such scarcity, rather than driving up the value of the uncirculated scholarship, renders it worthless as a medium of international currency. Here is where ephemerality exacts a heavy toll on African literary research: the scholar publishes, but his ideas almost instantly perish. Yet these elite and highly obscure official media somehow linger on, invisible vestigial organs still necessary to the functioning of the internal workings of the academic body.

But before we get too morbid about all this, perhaps we need to remind ourselves that little magazines, despite their small size and circumscribed circulation, can have an immense impact on a fledgling literary culture, especially one that hasn't yet managed to get completely off the ground. This happened not so long ago in Malawi, just as it had in Nigeria and Kenya years earlier, so let us turn our attention briefly to Zomba, where Chancellor College, alias the University of Malawi, is located. Chancellor College has the distinction of having been home to one of the longest-running undergraduate magazines in anglophone Africa, a mimeographed English Department broadsheet called *The Muse* (which is not to be confused with an even longer-running albeit irregular literary journal of the same name published at the University of Nigeria). By 1986 *The Muse* was in its thirteenth year, having put out more than ninety issues, and was still going strong. It had been founded by Ken Lipenga and two other undergraduates as an outlet for student writing, and every bit of the production work on it—editing, typing, proofreading, distribution—has always been done by students. As Lipenga (who used to teach Chancellor College) explained in an interview,

> *The Muse*, though always run by students, has been open to anybody interested in contributing. It was actually meant to be an extension of the Writers' Workshop [a weekly forum for discussion of writing done by students and faculty]. That's how we justified its establishment. There are times in the Writers' Workshop when you feel tongue-tied, overwhelmed by some superior voices, and you don't say anything; you are too shy to speak. *The Muse* then offers you an opportunity to express your views on the poem or short story that others were discussing. You have a chance, in other words, to put your views forward in another medium. Or there may be times, even after you have made your contribution to the discussion, when you feel there was something else you should have said, or something you could have said better. There is the opportunity to use *The Muse* to clarify your views, if you wish. So it has always been linked with the Writers' Workshop, and to this day *The Muse* still serves a useful purpose (15).

Several of the students and faculty who have actively participated in the Writers' Workshop and contributed literary pieces and commentary to *The Muse*—Felix Mnthali, Jack Mapanje, Steve Chimombo, Frank Chipasula, Paul Zeleza and Ken Lipenga himself, for example—went on to publish books of poetry and fiction and today are regarded as among the leading literary figures in the country.

But *The Muse* wasn't the only outlet open to them. *Odi*, a "bilingual quarterly of Malawian writing" that carried mostly verse and fiction, had been started on campus a few years earlier, as had a printed students' miscellany that subsequently came to be called *Umodzi*. Then *Denga*, a publication given over largely to reports on local theatrical productions, including those taken on tour by the university's traveling theater troupe, put in an appearance, and *Kalulu*, a "Bulletin of Oral Literature," was launched. *Outlook*, a "Bulletin of Language, Literature and Culture" sponsored by the English Department, also surfaced briefly and somewhat tentatively in the mid-1970s, but after its editor returned from study leave in the early 1980s, it rapidly gained weight, force and regularity. Next *Baraza*, a "Journal of the Arts in Malawi" that the university's Department of Fine and Performing Arts first produced in 1983 in a thin foolscap format, was transformed into a sleeker and more respectable-looking academic serial. *Kalulu, Outlook* and *Baraza* would have to be classified as scholarly rather than belletristic publications, but each has contributed in its own way to the enrichment of cultural life at the university. And collectively these ambitious faculty journals as well as the more cavalier student media have made Chancellor College one of the liveliest literary campuses on the entire continent. Malawi is a small country, and Chancellor College is not a large institution, but per capita there appears to have been more written by and for students there than at any other African university. These academic little magazines have thus not just enhanced student life but have raised significantly the whole nation's level of creative self-expression. There is nothing little about such a prodigious achievement.

Chancellor College is not the only African university campus where sustained investment in campus publications has yielded impressive dividends. One sees the same process going on in enlightened literature departments at other tertiary institutions, particularly at Ahmadu Bello University in northern Nigeria, where three fine journals are published by the English Department: *Kuka*, "a Journal of Creative and Critical Writing," formerly called *The Mirror*; *Saiwa*, a "Journal of Communication"; and *Work in Progress*, a faculty journal of literary research and opinion. Another example worth mentioning is the University of Yaoundé, which has produced *Abbia* (now defunct), *New Horizons, Ngam, Mould, Syllabus, African Theatre Review*, and the *Union of African Performing Artists News*. One hopes that such imaginative ventures in translating thought into print will not only increase and multiply throughout the African continent but will also spread well beyond the narrow confines of the individual campuses that generate them, leading to a much wider cross-fertilization of ideas internationally. African little magazines, easily exploitable resources with enormous potential, deserve to grow much bigger in the future.

[1] For further information on both journals, see Benson.

Armah's Achimota Writings

Ayi Kwei Armah's five novels have been very carefully scrutinized in books by Robert Fraser, Derek Wright, Neil Lazarus and K. Damodar Rao and in critical articles by scores of African and non-African scholars. A few of these studies have taken into account the early short fiction Armah contributed not only to African magazines such as *The New African, Okyeame* and *Présence Africaine*, but also, following publication of *The Beautyful Ones Are Not Yet Born* in 1968, to such mainstream Western media as *Atlantic Monthly* and *Harper's Magazine*. The earliest of this "apprenticeship fiction" (Wright 1989: 17)[1] to reach print was "Contact," a story of an interracial sexual misadventure in the United States which came out in *The New African* in December 1965, when Armah was twenty-six years old. The tale is interesting as a precursor to *Why Are We So Blest?*, a novel in which Armah expanded upon a similarly entwined triple theme of racial, political and sexual exploitation. It was no doubt Armah's years of residence and education in the United States, first at Groton School in 1959-60 and then as an undergraduate at Harvard University in 1960-63, that led him to explore such themes with so much intensity and insight.

But Armah's period of apprenticeship as a writer really began several years before he left Ghana. The earliest published traces of his scribblings found so far date back to 1957, the year of Ghana's independence, when he was a Form VI student at Achimota, Ghana's top secondary boarding school. Armah's parents, both of whom were teachers, had sent him to primary schools in Sekondi and Cape Coast between 1945 and 1951, and he must have displayed unusual academic ability at an early age, for when he went on to Achimota in 1952, he was granted a Common Entrance Bursary Award every year he was in the lower Forms (1952-56), and during that period he certainly lived up to his promise, winning Form prizes in his first, second and fifth years, first prize in the Form VI Arts entrance exam, and a Form VI Scholarship Award for 1957-58. In addition, he garnered the Achimota Special Literature Contest Prize in 1956; earned a first-grade Cambridge School Certificate that same year with distinctions in English Language, English Literature, Geography, Latin and Science, and credits in French, History and Mathematics; and attained his West African Higher School Certificate in 1958 after taking Form VI subject prizes in English, Geography and Latin. It is not surprising that when he moved on to Groton School on full scholarship, he graduated *magna cum laude* and gained admittance to Harvard on an honorary national scholarship.

However, he wasn't just a successful swot. He also participated actively in extra-curricular activities, especially sports (cricket, field hockey, soccer, swimming, table tennis, tennis, volleyball), drama, and school publications. In his final years at Achimota he served as a writer and director of house and school plays, as editor of a house newspaper, as secretary of the School Prefectorial Council, and as editor and then editor-in-chief of the school magazine. In addition he took on various student administrative responsibilities: house librarian, house monitor, house representative to the school library committee, and house prefect. At Groton he maintained his involvement in publications, serving on the editorial board for the school magazine.[2]

In this latter respect Armah was no different from his literary predecessors and peers elsewhere in anglophone Africa, for it was in school magazines that many of them got their first glimpse of their own words in print. Chinua Achebe, Wole Soyinka, Ngugi wa Thiong'o—to name only the most illustrious pioneers—were active contributors to such vehicles in their schooldays and persisted in writing for and/or editing campus publications at the universities they attended. School magazines gave them all their start; it was by regularly producing materials for their schoolmates to read that they began to conceive of themselves as publishing writers, as men of the pen.

The earliest of Armah's recovered schoolboy writings are four pieces in the 1958 issue of *The Achimotan*: an editorial, a miscellany of "School Notes," an essay questioning the appropriateness of the school's Latin motto "Ut Omnes Unum Sint?," and a three-and-a-half page poem entitled "Joseph's Fall." Three of these pieces are signed George Armah; the Latinate essay introduces a variation: G.A. Armah. Armah evidently did not change his pen name from George to Ayi Kwei until after he had lived in the United States for several years.

The Editorial, commenting in general on the contents of the 1958 issue of *The Achimotan*, offers some good-natured but slightly mischievous teasing of girls at the school for not doing their share in providing articles for the school magazine:

We do not know how the school is going to receive this year's *Achimotan*. Certainly, there is bound to be a great deal of controversy between the sexes, and it would be interesting to know what boys and girls think about those articles that are likely to raise special anger or malicious glee, depending of course, on one's sex. The impartial observer will perhaps conclude, after reading this volume, that our girls seem to have fared the worse in the great controversy, and one cannot help feeling sorry for them, and wishing they would speak up much more than they are content to do at present, for the apparent inability of girls to write for the school magazine, or their contemptuous apathy towards doing so, is most regrettable. There are normally two girls on the Editorial Board and three boys. The scanty arithmetical skill of even the most obtuse Arts Student is therefore quite enough to make it clear that one might expect to find two articles by girls to every three by boys—if girls were willing to write. As every Kwaku, Kojo and Kwaw can see, this is not so—at all, and it's a great pity.

We only hope that it is from natural feminine diffidence and not any insuperable biological reason that girls have hitherto refrained from honouring the pages of the *Achimotan* with the fruits of their erudition, and that henceforth, prompted perhaps by the heavy-handedness of the cruder sex, they will step out of their simulated ignorance of the fact that girls too can write, and repudiate Balzac's saying, that 'the first condition of learning in the woman is that the fact should be kept a strict secret.' After all, writing being the refined art it is, is it not fitting that it should most concern the fairer sex?

One does not know where Armah picked up the provocative quote from Balzac, but his reference to writing being a "refined art" is worthy of note, this editorial being a splendid example of the art of refined needling.

Armah's "School Notes" record the highs and lows of the preceding school year, 1957, when the Gold Coast became independent Ghana. Naturally there was a lot of excitement in the air, but some hopes, as Armah notes, were doomed to disappointment:

Without meaning to boast, every Achimotan will assert that Achimota begat Ghana. It was therefore a matter of course that we here expected to be direct participants in the lion's share of the festivities. In anticipation of the pomp surrounding a royal visit to our campus, decorators had made the school pleasingly bright. Old-looking buildings were given a face lift; expert hedge-trimmers excelled themselves to give our hedges that famous controlled look; an army of labourers was kept extremely busy doing various chores.

After all this activity, then, the knowledge that the Duchess of Kent and her royal party were not, after all, visiting this school because of a tailored schedule, was no inconsiderable disappointment. We took it, however, in excellent spirit, and went, since the Duchess would not come to see us, to see her at the College Oval. This unfortunate disappointment apart, we celebrated our Independence fittingly. Students who could afford to go to their parents were allowed to, and those of us who remained on the compound had an enjoyable time at our House feasts, and we were admirably consoled by the presence of the Frasers and the American Vice-President Mr. Nixon with us.

It is of course understandable that young Achimotans would have preferred to consort with the Duchess of Kent rather than with Richard Nixon, who even then was not much of a consolation prize.

The other disappointing news of the year was that "incredible though it may sound, we failed to qualify for the Boys' Athletic finals," due in part to the condition of the arena at Kibi which "must have been the very thing in Bunyan's mind when he wrote of the Slough of Despond, it being an unpleasant compromise between a football field and a Swimming Pool." But school spirit was not entirely dampened by such setbacks, for there were offsetting gains in other areas. Armah reported with some pride that the Founders' Day Pageant was "unexcelled in the School, having as its highlights, a masque produced by Miss Bently and Mr. Sherwood"; that "Mr. Berriman, a new master [in charge of dramatic productions] has shown himself a master artist, able to work wonders with scenery and the stage in general"; that a new inter-house competition in general knowledge "has been very diverting" even though received by "the great part of the student body" with "apparent apathy"; and that a new electronic organ installed in the Assembly Hall has "lent a hitherto lacking sweetness to hymn singing at Protestant Services." Armah nonetheless felt compelled to draw an appropriate moral lesson for those of his fellow students who were beginning to manifest symptoms of academic complacency and idleness:

> It sounds like preaching, to tell students that perfection must be striven for, imagination developed and industry cultivated. I believe the exhortation has been worn blunt by endless repetition; it is nonetheless true. If we are to maintain our high standards year after difficult year, we need not only to recognise the fact that industry pays, but to act on our recognition.

In other words, talented students should discipline themselves to be the very best that they can be; the beautiful ones must struggle to be born.

Armah's essay "Ut Omnes Unum Sint?" questioned the veracity of the school motto "That all may be one" by pointing to signs of disunity rather than unity, inequality rather than equality, at Achimota. These signs were to be found not in relations between black and white—that is, between Achimota's students and faculty—but in relations between students of different gender. Here Armah returned to the theme of his Editorial:

The fact is, that there is an enormous amount of hostility between Achimota's boys and girls. It is difficult to find a reason for this unhappy state of affairs. One would think that recent developments in the school's administrative policies would make for better relations between the sexes; it is doubtful whether the reverse is not now happening. Boys mix with girls in the Dining Hall, with the result that boys have had to change their gastronomic habits considerably. Formerly, hidden safely in the "Zongo" sections of the Dining Hall—the part near the present High Table—boys could happily shovel huge quantities of food into their insides without being laughed at. It is a patent fact that our girls are addicted to giggling, fits of which are brought on by the sight of the businesslike way in which boys tackle their food. It is no less well-established that the Achimota male does not like being giggled at. What happens then, when boys shovel and girls giggle, is a sort of mild atomic explosion, usually triggered by the boy, whose fallout embroils the girl's friends, sometimes whole groups, or even Houses of girls, in bitter feuds with the corresponding entourages supporting the boy. The girls draw their breath in between molars and premolars when they see the boys, or, more effectively, all burst out into thunderous laughter when they see any of the boys, causing untold misery and much loss of appetite. Talking at table is restricted to spasmodic hot debates on whether this fellow acted well in trying to slap that girl, etc. In these debates the sexes are always cleanly divided, girls supporting girls and boys boys. The odd boy out who speaks out for the weaker sex is suspected of casting his bread on the waters, perhaps in preparation for an 'application' and is usually ostracised unofficially by his colleagues.

Armah does not offer a solution to this all-consuming battle of the sexes, saying instead that "This is the first of a series of studies on this sociological problem." But unlike the approach he adopted in his Editorial, here he teases boys as well as girls. The laugh is on everybody.

Armah's long poem on "Joseph's Fall" is worth quoting in full, if only to illustrate his virtuosity in handling metrical language (mostly iambic pentameter) and achieving a mock romantic idiom:

> On Achimota's hills are houses nine;
> Of these but three must harbour girls; the rest,
> All six of them, are crammed with boys—and men.
> Which dire inequity is magnified
> By that the three each hold less than the six.
> What consequences dire this means, and what
> Disasters grim, I sing.
>
> There was a boy.
> His name was Joseph, oft clip'd to Joe.
> In Livingstone's blest House he liv'd a life
> Of simplest scholarship. Awake at 6,
> Fast toilet when t'was warm, to Congo when
> T'was cold; then up to chapel there to sing
> His harsh falsetto, noting not the looks
> Oblique of those who felt him out of tune.
> In class no Sputnik he; yet was he not
> A dunce outright. He might be worse than those
> Blest students, doom'd to constantly deserve
> Their hard won nines—But he was better far
> Than all that host of bombing studentry
> That scarcely breath'd for once above a three.
> Content, revolving around the customed five,

He joy'd when, glad surprise, he scored a six,
And philosophic eyed the sad mark, four.
So that, in all particulars this Joe
Was what I said he was: to all intents
An Ordinary Boy.

He had a bosom friend,
To whom for the purpose of this narrative
We'll give the name of Bob. Between the two
Of them was known the existence of a love
As dear as Jonathan for David bore.
To Bob, t'was pleasure just to be with Joe,
And ever more he looked for ways to do him good.
One day, while walking to the Dining Hall,
Bob saw—heart-cheering sight—a beauteous girl.
It chanced that she behind our Joseph walk'd,
Apparently engrossed in every move
That Joe might make. This our friend Bob perceived,
And quick to seek th'advantage amical,
Call'd Joe soon as the meal was done and said:
My dearest Joe, I have some news for you;
Please listen patiently, and when I've done,
You'll promise me to do whate'er I say.
This morning, as we near'd the Dining Hall
I saw a sight: you walk'd before a girl,
To wit, Patricia Sey. And while you walked
She looked at you, your every motion, yes,
With such apparent love, that straight I knew
She was as good as yours. The hour has struck,
And now's your chance to woo the girl: he said.
Now Bob had placed his bosom friend between
A heaven and a Hell, for Joe knew well
That what appears as interest in girls
Is often nothing more than anxiousness.
He had misgivings, nay, pangs premonitory,
And nearly spoke against the plan, but when
His friend in serious argument had proved
Its case, at length did he consent to have his Bob

As Catalyst.

The stage was set, the piece
Rehearsed, Joe was completely different.
His hitherto indifferent self had been
O'erswamp'd and banished clean. Meticulous
In all extreme, Joe had become to all intents
A proper dandy boy. His clothes he washed
Himself with Surf, and ironed twice a day.
Where in the past, he'd always been content
To clean his mouth dotch-oiled, by rubbing same
With turn'd up collar of his shirt, he now
Maintained a formidable fleet, no less,
Of seven beauteous dear-bought handkerchiefs.
His morsels in the Dining Hall which erst
Were shovelled, indiscriminate of rice or dotch
With large dimensions, frightful to behold,
Now shrivelled up. Each midget morsel now
Had half a minute's sojourn in his jaws,
Where hitherto none was allowed to last four secs.
Joe's steps, whenever he walked in places where
His lady might be near, were measured, nice,
And taken in even time. In short, the change
That came o'er Joe was so complete, entire,
That all did wonder mightily.

Meanwhile Bob laid foundations wide. Whenever he
Had seen the girl he'd said a fervent pray'r
On Joe's behalf. Reporting all to Joe, he changed
All no's to 'Nothing said the girl,' and Hmms
to yeses definite. So Joe was made to think
Success would come.

A rendezvous was fix'd,
The time agreed upon; that eve did Joseph
Wear his best attire, white-white, with tie
And blazer too. T'was supper's end, Joseph stood
And waited for the girl. She came, but not,

As Joe expected, with any thought of love.
As soon as she had stormed within his hearing,
She shouted out: "Bob says you want to speak
To me, What's it, Please Hurry up, I want
To join my friends." Then Joseph, somewhat coold'
Made Remonstration meet. 'Please don't be cross
I want to tell you, er, I mean—ehem—;
'Well look,' replied the girl, I'm late, if you
Will nothing say but stand and hem and moan,
I'll have to go!'

At this did Joseph seize
Her arm. He tried to keep his eyes on hers
But, feeling somewhat foolish, cast them down.
He spoke—a high falsetto speech, which
Made the girl quite laugh, though she
Was evidently sore: 'I love you, dear.'
She sneered, and Joseph cursed within his mind.
He would have something said, but that the girl
Went off, with nothing like Goodnight.
That night Joe could not dream or even sleep.
He turned it over in his mind, ransacked
His brain for hopeful words whereon to hang
A hope. But no! Think how he might, the fact
Remained: The girl had said 'At all'.

                                    Days passed.

And merged themselves in weeks. Four weeks had passed
And Joseph still remembered how he'd fail'd.
Still was he Robert's friend, but in their midst
Had crept a sort of feeling suspicious; not trusting each,
They each knew not what thought the other boy.
Joe felt Bob laughed to think how he was duped;
Bob thought Joe felt he was to blame.
Meanwhile did Joseph suffer grim uneasiness
Where late he'd feigned a squeamish appetite,
He now did lose it quite; His bones stuck out,
He gave allowance negligent to beard

And mustacios. His shaggy face was sad,
His hair unkempt. His eyes grew wild,
And his attention wandered all the time,
And aye he brooded over this. That girls
All being what they were, would laugh at him.
And make his life a hell. But all must have
An end; although in our disasters amorous
The end takes long to come. Though 'tis a long,
Long time since he his red hibiscus got,
He even now doth feel a pang, whenever
This flower, this spoiler of the student's peace,
Doth come into his sight.

"There is a comfort in the strength of love
'Twill make a thing endurable which else
Would overset the brain or break the heart,"
Said William Wordsworth, who could not have put
Joe's case more succinctly. He loves the girl,
Still does, but when he thinks her charms o'er now,
He doesn't overlook the minus quantities, as when
He first became inflamed. She said "At all".
God bless her for she's left the boy in peace.

This almost sounds like a parody of Chaucer's "Troilus and Criseyde" except that here Troilus fails at lovemaking, Pandarus fails at pandering, and Criseyde fails at acknowledging, much less alleviating, her suitor's suffering. It's the old "mismatched sexes" theme again, but this time the fool is an Ordinary Boy who allows himself to be ensnared by a romantic fantasy. Armah is lightheartedly burlesquing the trauma of unrequited puppy love. As a teenager he seems to have taken pleasure in highlighting some of the absurdities arising from the awkwardness of boy-girl relationships. This was a far cry from his obsession with the cruel brutality of sexual politics in later works such as "Contact" and *Why Are We So Blest?* At Achimota he wrote far more innocently of gender conflicts.

A second set of Armah's adolescent compositions can be found in the 1959 issue of *The Achimotan*. This time there was a team-written Editorial, another miscellany of "School Notes," a report on Livingstone House (where Armah served as House Prefect), and a humorous essay entitled "One Up or How to Be Somebody," which was modeled on the "One-Upmanship" lampoons of Stephen Potter.

The Editorial begins by announcing an important reform in this year's school magazine:

> Last year's Achimotan was born under a not very lucky star. Acts of God conspired to delay its final issue, and when it did come out it sparked off a sharp intersex war that lasted for many weeks...But in the end the choler subsided, and the Editorial Board's recrudescent appeals for material brought in an appreciable number of articles...Too much emphasis can be, and probably of late has been, laid on the fact that Achimota consists of two sex blocs whose peaceful coexistence is often on the brink of destruction. We have tacitly concluded therefore that this dog has been worked overtime, and have decided to let it lie slumbering.

Another reform announced by the Editorial Board concerned policing itself against possible abuse of office:

> Further, a sort of ladies and gentlemen's agreement has been arrived at requiring that NO member of the Board should ever be awarded the prize for the year's best article. We have found this necessary not because we consider our own ethical standards faulty (for the board is made up of honourable men and women), but because it is desirable to insure against the possibility itself of selfishness, advertent or otherwise.

One wonders if such self-regulation by the Board might not have been directed at Armah himself, one of the school's top prize-winners. There may be some significance in the fact that this Editorial was drafted by the entire editorial board, not just by

Armah alone. Perhaps his fellow editors were trying to rein him in.

Armah's "School Notes" chronicled the highlights of the preceding year, which included a one-day visit by six British students, three boys and three girls, who "had the opportunity to dine, worship, mix and go to classes with us." They had enjoyed the high life dances, the Ghanaian clothing they were given, and the natural warmth of bath and swimming pool water.

> The group had been struck too by the general friendliness shown them, and before leaving, assured us that they would try to eradicate the impression, still rife in some European circles, that Africa is the exclusive property of apes and tigers and crocodiles tolerating, in occasional pockets of human habitation, little groups of savages, by no means always noble.

Armah went on to report that 1958 had been a good year for school theatrical productions; one house had put on a "tragi-comico-musical hotch-potch" featuring "a group of Rock'n'Rollers [who] started quite a lively interest in this art of pelvic gyration." It had been a good year for sports too, "practically ...the Annus Mirabilis for boys, though one would hesitate to be so enthusiastic about the girls' achievements. From somewhere near last in athletics, we rocketed into first place, far, far away from the sweating atmosphere surrounding the other schools struggling to get hold of our shoelaces." The football team had also done well, losing not a single school match once boots were banned as harmful "Footballistic Weapons." On the gastronomic front the Dining Hall chalked up a mixed year of gains and losses, its "fossilized" menu undergoing only modest renovation:

> Horlicks looked, for one breathless week, like replacing the ancient and well tried cocoa, but though it put up a fierce fight, mustering behind itself the support of many pleased plates, it succumbed at last in a technical K.O. to the now experienced defending champion,

Cocoa. The school's performance in academics, however, showed a decline: "For last year's School Certificate, out of 97 candidates, 9 failed. The Higher School Certificate was rather worse, 9 people failing out of a total of 45."

Armah's "Livingstone House" report registered a similar assortment of wins and losses in sports and singing competitions, but overall some progress was visible: "Until this year, there was a strong belief that the very composition of Livingstone's masonry precluded the possibility of any sports trophies finding their way in. Our Seniors have now deflated this taboo."

Armah's eight-page essay on "One Up or How to Be Somebody," the longest piece he ever prepared for *The Achimotan*, retained the same light tone and bemused acuity of observation that characterized his other schoolboy writings. The problem it addressed was one of asserting individuality within a community: specifically, how could a student at Achimota, one in a herd of six hundred dressed in school uniform, make himself more conspicuous? How could he distinguish himself from others and be somebody? Armah then identified the sciences that students at Achimota had developed to cope with this problem:

1. Dandymanship: an "exacting science," the aim of which is "perfection in clothes and demeanour." It requires "getting two sets of uniform in excess of the normal number," ironing shirts and shorts every day and "even between periods, if possible," and shaming scruffier-looking students by loudly lamenting how dirty and crumpled up the Dandyman's own immaculate apparel has become.

2. Stuffmanship: this science requires giving the appearance of not studying yet doing well in all academic work, absorbing knowledge as if by osmosis. "Stuffmen are constantly required to feign surprise, since they turn out to have high marks in exams for which they swear they have learnt nothing."

3. Impressionmanship: "a science by which the student, without really being any better than any of his contemporaries,

can get his Masters into a condition in which they will be prepared to lay down their lives in defence of his transcendent wit." This can be done by impressing teachers with one's range of irrelevant knowledge or by using terminology the teachers themselves are not likely to know. The best Impressionmen "learn just enough advanced stuff to convince masters they are ahead of everybody else, including, in some respects the masters themselves."

4. Comfymanship: this "entails doing the most unpleasant things very well, and pretending you are enjoying them no end; things like getting up at about 5.20 a.m. and doing curatorial work, and never going late to any place. That, of course, is just the basis. The high stuff includes gambits like sprinting towards some mistress laden with books, and, still panting heroically, offering, preferably with a Latin Lover sort of deep bow, to transport her cargo, be it into nethermost regions of Hades, or, even further, to the Form One Block."

5. Rock'n'Roll Manship: a minor but "popular science nowadays" requiring tapping one's feet vigorously, closing one's eyes, and shouting out a few bars of the hottest Rock'n'Roll tunes, but avoiding dancing for this would clearly reveal the extent of one's real ignorance of this type of music.

6. Dotchmanship: a science of securing the largest and softest "elephant" portions available in the Dining Hall pan without giving the appearance of being concerned to do so. "Dotchmanship is guaranteed to bring fame. It has the great advantage of not needing anything special except a capacious stomach."

This is fairly typical schoolboy humor, focusing on food, fads and false appearances. Armah's competitive spirit, emphasis on individualism, and concern with excelling even in these rather dubious "sciences" may signal something deeper, however: a desire, even in jest, to stand out, to shine, to manifest brilliance or attain an extraordinary success. Armah, as a student, appears to have been strongly motivated to excel at whatever he did. He may have been a compulsive overachiever, always reaching well beyond the range of what others could readily grasp. He sought not just to be better than most of schoolmates; he wanted to be the very best of all.

From the samples we have seen it is obvious that he was a precociously gifted writer. His control of syntax, suppleness of style, ample vocabulary, learned allusions, and complete mastery of idiomatic expressions—in short, his sheer eloquence—were of a very high order indeed, far higher than one might be entitled to expect from even the most advanced secondary school graduates. He had a special talent that was already becoming fully developed, so much so that he appeared destined to become a powerful writer.

He also gave the impression of being emotionally well-balanced. Nearly all of the writing he did for *The Achimotan* was humorous, but his was a gentle sort of humor, never vicious or harshly satirical. In those days he laughed wholeheartedly, all the while gaining a reputation for impish wit and stylistic cleverness. He had an eye for incongruity and a resiliently optimistic outlook on life. He seemed to be enjoying himself immensely.

So it must have been his years in the United States that changed Armah from a happy, successful, well-adjusted schoolboy to a disillusioned, dissatisfied, disgruntled young adult. He could still write brilliantly, but his youthful ebullience had been tempered by bitter experiences and menacing thoughts. The few critics who have commented on his earliest published short fiction have characterized it as "sad and pessimistic in tone" (Ker 15) and as reflecting a brooding concern with "an unchanging cycle of exploitative and frustrating dependency" (Wright 1989: 33); these were dark little tales that, in mood and atmosphere, anticipated the existential gloom permeating his first three novels. He continued to write about false appearances, institutionalized social inequities, and gender conflicts—some of the same themes that had animated his carefree Achimota juvenilia—but his writing now was marked by a mercilessly sardonic inflection, a revulsion against things as they were.

Within a few short years Armah had been transformed into Africa's angriest young author.[3]

---

[1] For further analysis of Armah's early fiction, see Wright 1985 and 1990.

[2] These biographical details have been gleaned from an appendix to Ezugu which appears to have been based on a copy of Armah's curriculum vitae.

[3] I wish to express my gratitude to James Gibbs for supplying me with photocopies of Armah's writings in *The Achimotan*.

Book Publishing at Home and Abroad

ators

$15/d - 1875)/3^2$

Romances for the Office Worker: Aubrey Kalitera and Malawi's White-Collar Reading Public

Modern African literature first became known to the outside world through the works of elite, university-educated writers published in Europe and America. To be sure, there had been a few exceptions such as Amos Tutuola and Cyprian Ekwensi, authors whose craftsmanship had not been molded, polished and refined by years of literary education in colonial schools and universities, but these were freaks by any standard, sports of nature whose ungainly blemishes were their chief source of interest to a Western reading public. It had been the Senghors, Diops, Layes, Betis and Oyonos, the Achebes, Soyinkas, Ngugis, Armahs and Mphahleles who had made the greatest impact on the international scene, for they had demonstrated through the force and sophistication of their art that Africa in the postwar era could speak quite eloquently for itself, interpreting its own experience in its own idiom, albeit in a European tongue. These highbrow writers produced the first permanent flowers in what was to become a lush tropical garden of literature; they were exotic hothouse plants that abruptly assumed gigantic proportions, making themselves conspicuous as much by their unexpected weight and bulk as by their dazzling variety of shapes and colors. No one had anticipated such a sudden riot of creativity.

But in the environments from which some of them had sprung there had existed prior to their efflorescence a profuse undergrowth of literary vitality expressing itself in humbler but nonetheless significant forms. This was particularly true in the anglophone territories, where writing in vernacular languages had been encouraged. Behind and beneath Soyinka, for instance, there had been a rich legacy of written literature in Yoruba, ranging from poetry and mythic narratives to episodic folkloric fantasies and detective novels. In Ngugi's formative background there had been a small anticolonial pamphlet literature in Gikuyu and a very large popular and religious literature in Kiswahili. Mphahlele had had access to a full century of school storybooks published in South African Bantu languages.

But indigenous creativity did not confine itself to mother tongues. In Nigeria the earliest Onitsha market chapbooks, produced largely in English and to a lesser extent in Igbo, antedated Achebe's first novels by more than a decade, and in Ghana a similar tradition of pamphlet romances in English prepared the ground for Armah's initial anti-romantic fictions. In South Africa, Mphahlele was stimulated a great deal by the racy township potboilers he read and edited for *Drum* magazine; some of the stylistic gusto of this brand of pulp fiction rubbed off on his own journalism, autobiographical memoirs, novels and short stories.

So the splendid flowering of African literature that surprised the world did not take place in a complete literary vacuum, at least not in anglophone Africa. There was already a rich compost of prior creativity out of which it emerged and defined itself. The elite writers, by reaching for the sun, may have earned the greatest glory, but the popular writers, by spreading themselves laterally rather than vertically, may have reached the widest audience.

And the populists have never been totally eclipsed or displaced by the literati. Indeed, there probably are more popular writers (i.e., authors who address themselves to the common reader in their own society rather than to intellectuals at home or abroad) in anglophone Africa today than there are elite writers, and collectively, and in a few cases individually, they may have cornered a larger share of the indigenous reading public than all but the biggest giants whose works are compulsory reading in schools and universities. The mass appeal of lowbrow scribblers such as Cyprian Ekwensi of Nigeria and David Maillu of Kenya is already well-known and well-documented. The popular writer I wish to draw attention to here comes from a much smaller country, Malawi, and has not yet attracted much attention elsewhere. But in Malawi Aubrey Kalitera is famous and in all likelihood is more widely read than any other Malawian author. His career offers some interesting insights into what it takes to survive and thrive as a writer for the masses in a small country.

I first became aware of Kalitera when I visited Malawi in 1986 and saw on the bookshelves of colleagues at Chancellor College, University of Malawi, a number of curious paperback books of crude design and rough construction. On closer inspection I noticed that the text in these books was not set in type but appeared to be reproduced from ordinary typewriting on a rather antiquated office machine. The covers had bold, stenciled lettering and sometimes carried simple illustrations. The volumes were fairly sturdily bound and ran to about 400 pages each. Most were novels but a few were collections of short stories, all written by a single author, Aubrey Kalitera, and published by a firm that called itself Power Pen Books. I had not seen such works in any of the local bookshops, so I asked where I could obtain copies. "Oh, you'll have to see Kalitera himself," I was told. "He not only writes them but also manufactures and sells them."

Kalitera lived in Blantyre, so I made a point of contacting him when I passed through that city a few days later. We met and chatted for about an hour. Here are some of the things he told me about himself:

> One disadvantage I had in life is that I didn't have much schooling. I lost my father when I was very young—when I was ten—so I didn't have much formal schooling. When I sat down to write, it was out of frustration. I simply had nothing to do. When you are in the village, all you can do is go to your garden in the morning. Well, you toil, then you come back at about 10 or 11, and unless possibly you go out hunting, you've got nothing to do. If you've

had a little education, you may want to express it. That's all. That is the way it started.

Almost twenty years ago—I think I was sixteen—I thought possibly I could play with writing. Gradually I got attached to it, but it took me something like ten years to publish my first book, *A Taste of Business*, which came out in Nairobi. Then a year later I followed it up with *A Prisoner's Letter*...What I was trying to do was to write for an international publisher. When I wrote my books, I used to send them to London. I sent this book, *A Taste of Business*, to Heinemann in London and they forwarded it to their office in Kenya. That's what happened.

When I started to write, there was only one man who had written a real book here: that was Aubrey Kachingwe. Most of the writers I was reading were foreign...When I thought I had the ability to write, I had a dream of being able to live on my writing. But those two books I published in Kenya sort of disillusioned me; I realized I wasn't going to be able to live on my writing if I continued to publish with someone else. I had this feeling that if I could publish my own books and sell them myself, possibly I would get a living out of them. I had no money. In fact, I had nothing, so I picked up an old duplicating machine and then bought some stencils. Somewhere along the line I had learned to type very well, so I typed my own stencils. After that, I bought a bit of paper, ran possibly one hundred and twenty copies, and then sold them by hand.

Before I went into book publication, I was running a short story magazine called *Sweet Mag*. When I began, I printed a thousand copies, but then, alas, it was a new thing and was almost valueless. People were not looking at it, so I was not very careful with the copies. But then after two or three months people began wanting the copies.

I wrote the stories. It was ABC. Writing then was very easy. I started by producing a thousand copies, but when they didn't all sell, I produced only five hundred the next week. Those I did manage to sell. By the following week, there was a greater demand, so I went back to a thousand, then fifteen hundred. I think I did seventeen hundred at one point...

I marketed them just by selling them around here in Blantyre. I didn't go to other cities. I think the price was thirty tambala and later forty tambala. I was just taking them around to shops, around to offices. People were buying them like that. Then I'd go back home, write some more, and in the mornings take them out again for selling...

So I started as a short story magazine publisher, and I was writing all the stories myself. As a matter of fact, one of my books, *She Died in My Bed*, is just a compilation of some of the short stories I had written. A few of my other books are also compilations of some of those stories in *Sweet Mag*. When I started doing these books, people came to know me as a writer and began asking, "Why did you start?" When they heard there had been a magazine, they said, "Now we want those stories," so I had no choice. By then the magazines had been thrown away, so the only way I could actually reproduce them was to put them out in book form...

If I remember right, I think I wrote at least one book before I started writing these stories. I didn't know how to get it published, so after some time I went ahead and published it myself. I thought I would do both the magazine and the books, but being single-handed, I found it impossible. I dropped the magazine and went ahead with the books. The magazine stopped about the time the books got started...

As a matter of fact, producing books that way was very cheap because stencils are cheap; they're just about the cheapest way of printing, only the quality is very poor. But in this case, the people were glad to see something that had been done locally. Also, some people said the books were well written, so actually they were buying them very quickly...

I was printing about six hundred a month at that time. First, I would produce six hundred copies of a new book; then the following month I would produce possibly three hundred of that book and three hundred of another book. There were times when the number of copies per month was running up to a thousand. Selling them wasn't a problem. The people liked the writing and were very eager to get them...

I was able to survive till I made a business mistake. When I was doing my own selling—that is, when I myself was going around to offices and selling the books—I was able to generate an income of something like a thousand kwacha a month. Then I said to myself, "Possibly I could double or triple this by employing other hands to help me." So I had some people come in to do the cutting of the stencils. Then I brought in some more people to do the running of the duplicator and the binding, and finally I hired something like twenty people to go round and sell the books across the entire country. That was a business mistake, because when those people went out to sell the books, some of them never came back with the money. So that was a big business mistake.

I was writing these books as I went along, and I would publish a book the moment it was completed. To me, writing wasn't difficult. It was comparatively easy for me to produce a book. As a matter of fact, what actually got me to stop was my awareness that I wasn't getting my money back. So I said, "Let me reorganize the whole thing." The last book I wrote is still not published, and it was ready about a year and a half ago. Now I've got an idea of taking my books to the conventional bookshops, but in order to do this, I've got to bring them to an acceptable quality. There's an organization here in Malawi called SEDOM—Small Enterprise Development Organization of Malawi—which actually bought an offset printing machine for me for that purpose. I'm trying to get all my books typeset professionally now, the old ones as well as the new ones. I will have the books printed professionally, and then I will go and dump them in bookshops and see if they will sell. Obviously they will go at a much slower pace than I was able to achieve by selling them from office to office, because there is no way you can move a thousand copies of any book in this country. The market is very small. You can't sell that many copies in the bookshops.

I don't know how I can break into the outside market, but if the market is there, obviously I would be prepared to go and dump a few copies abroad. But I'm a simple man. As I said earlier on, I didn't have much formal schooling so there are a lot of things I don't know. I don't think it's going to be very easy for me to break into outside markets, but eventually possibly I'll do it. (Kalitera 3-9)

This interview was conducted in July of 1986, and since then no new books have rolled off the stencil sheets or offset printing equipment at Power Pen Books; but, according to a letter, Kalitera intended in 1989 to reprint in a more professional format his most successful earlier title, *Why Father Why*, and in the meantime had taken up an entirely new enterprise—filmmaking. In fact, in late 1988 he produced Malawi's first locally made feature film, *To Ndirande Mountain With Love*, which was based on one of the novels he wrote, published and peddled in 1983. Unfortunately, this new effort in reaching a mass audience was not commercially successful, but Kalitera gave it his best effort, investing his energy and entrepreneurial skill in attempting to make it succeed. He is a bold risk-taker, but not everything he touches turns into gold— or even copper, for that matter.

To date Kalitera has published at least eight novels and two collections of short stories. With the exception of the first two novels, *A Taste of Business* and *A Prisoner's Letter*, which were published in Nairobi in the late 1970s, all his books were brought out between September 1982 and the end of 1984 under the imprint of Power Pen Books. At that point he was producing a new book every three months. Prior to starting up *Sweet Mag* in January 1981, he had published a few of his short stories in *Malawi News* and had written at least one play and some stories for a local radio program called "Writer's Corner." *Sweet Mag* appears to have ceased publication in September 1983 when Kalitera was too busy as a book publisher to continue it.

Kalitera has always chosen themes for his novels that are of great interest to his readers. Many concern unfilial behavior. He writes about men who abandon their girlfriends after getting them pregnant, about women who abandon or kill their children in order to live a life of luxury unencumbered by parental responsibilities, about sons and daughters who desert or neglect their parents, about fathers and mothers who interfere in the marriages and romances of their grown-up children. But most of all he writes about marital infidelity, focusing on complications in the love affairs of men and women who cheat on their spouses or fiancées. Nearly all his narratives deal in one way or another with the making and breaking of contracts of the heart.

In these romantic melodramas the culprit often is a man whose biological instincts draw him irresistibly to beautiful women, most of whom ultimately yield to his persuasive advances. Men are seen as amorously gregarious and polygamous by nature; they are hunters always on the lookout for fresh prey. Women, on the other hand, though capable of being stirred by passions that override their inherent predisposition toward caution, tend to be more circumspect in making liaisons, looking for evidence of steadfastness, tenderness, and economic security. But they are vulnerable to flattery and the sheer libidinous persistence of their pursuers, and once they are won, they are quite prepared to take extraordinary risks to stick with their lover, even it if means leaving forever the contentment of a former way of life. They too can abandon themselves to the urgency of heartfelt emotions, but usually they are awakened receivers, not initiators, of erotic pressures.

Although love contracts are taken very seriously on both sides of the gender divide, they frequently are entered into in an abrupt, almost heedless manner. Love at first sight is common, the magnetic attraction generated at a random encounter proving impossible to suppress. The suddenness and intensity of this current of feeling overwhelm two strangers, and before long—certainly before marriage—they are strangers to one another no more, having found opportunities to sneak off to bed together to savor the sweetness of their reciprocal passion. Sometimes their quickly ignited sparks of love cool and die, for the man ordinarily cannot be depended upon to be forever constant, but more often than not the electricity of their connection holds them fast until they legitimize their union through marriage or until some tragedy finally separates them.

The marriage contract, however, is not as fixed and firm as the original love contract. Adulterous philandering is common, especially for the man, but this tends to be tolerated for the sake of maintaining the stability of the home and family. Sometimes, of course, great unhappiness ensues, culminating in divorce, murder, suicide or other desperate acts. The marriage contract, once abused, can be irrevocably shattered.

This is the stuff of romantic fiction all over the world, but Kalitera grounds his tales in a milieu that is unmistakably Malawian so his readers can easily identify with the men and women caught in these highly emotional entanglements. The landscape, the names, the material culture, the predicaments are all recognizably local, not foreign or exotic. There is also a fairly explicit message in some of the tales, giving even the most titillating of them a trace of traditional moral earnestness and the aura of a didactic parable or folktale. Kalitera, though operating in a popular medium of widespread international currency, still keeps his feet planted in his native soil.

A typical example of his moralistic manipulation of a popular romantic formula can be found in his first novella, *A Taste of Business*, which concerns the rise and fall of an adventurous small businessman. Ralph Namate, who has earned a business management diploma at a local polytechnic, is fed up with his junior executive position at an import/export firm, and wants to launch out on an entrepreneurial venture of his own in order to get "a taste of business." Since he lacks substantial start-up capital and marketing experience, his earliest forays into the fish business do not yield enough to satisfy his ambitions, but he is lucky enough to meet Della, a well-heeled airline stewardess who immediately falls for him and expresses her willingness to bankroll his smalltime enterprise. Though Ralph is more than willing to exploit Della sexually, he is reluctant initially to take her money, but eventually he not only borrows a small sum but also allows himself to be guided by her to better business opportunities. He sees her as a good-time girl, sugar mommy and potential spouse; she sees him as an investment for the future, telling him quite bluntly, "I won't make you a good wife unless you are a good businessman. You wouldn't satisfy me as a husband unless you are a good businessman" (67).

However, this well-calculated bond does not require that he remain faithful to her. Ralph does not hesitate to pick up an attractive undergraduate with whom he spends a four-day weekend at a fancy hotel, squandering his first major earnings. When Della finds out about the affair through her brother, who turns out to be the manager of the hotel, she confronts Ralph but is willing to accept his explanation that he was just obeying "the law of the three F's in action. Fool, fuck and forget" (64). However, she demands that he start to get serious about succeeding in business.

Ralph needs no further prompting. Following one of her business leads and displaying great ingenuity and courage on the job, he soon so distinguishes himself as a bigtime fish trader that the Chief Fisheries Officer at a lake research station notices him and arranges that he be offered a scholarship to go abroad to study for a B.Sc. with a major in fish handling and processing. But Della wants him to stay home and marry her; she is ready to settle down and cash in on her investment. Ralph now must choose between love and career, and when he disappoints Della again by flying off to London, she commits suicide by jumping off a bridge. Shaken, Ralph returns home and drops out of the fish business entirely. He has learnt his lesson.

The story is told by Ralph, who readily admits his weakness for beautiful women. Here is his account of his first encounter with Della:

> I will never even know what made me turn. All I can say is that I looked back down the queue and there she was. A woman so womanly, all woman—is the only way of describing her. Take it that God, by way of a demonstration to Jesus and the angels, made one model woman. Only one. That woman was Della...
>
> My reaction was purely reflex. We jump for our lives when we see a snake a foot from our feet. On the other hand, we men cannot help drawing close to a Della-ish woman. Seeing her, the feeling simply struck me that she was put in the world to be worshipped and to be given favours...(1)

> She was a woman who was all a man desired. Gentle and sweet. A woman, all woman. On top of that, educated. (4)

Five short, love-filled chapters later, he meets another girl whom he cannot resist:

> Well, honestly , when I left Zomba, I had fully intended to go and pick up Della for company. But on the Express, I met a Chancellor College lass called Memory. Boys will be boys! I felt I would have more fun with Memory than Della who I was beginning to take for granted now...(45)
>
> Memory and I laughed till our mouths hurt. We made love in every position in the book till our bodies felt worn. To put it all in a nutshell, I kept asking for more and more of Memory. Memory kept giving it till all self-control was over-ruled by passion, to borrow from Don Gibson's words. (46-47)

Ralph feels a bit ashamed of himself for having betrayed Della, but he justifies his conduct with the cavalier claim that "boys will be boys!"—a statement implying that all males observe the "law of three F's in action." Significantly, it is not his behavior in bed but his ambition in business that ultimately brings him low.

This is not to say that Kalitera fails to preach that irresponsible fornication is morally wrong. In certain circumstances, such as when the act produces offspring, the man is expected to honor the love bond by marrying his pregnant girlfriend. This is the message underscored time and again in the first novel Kalitera published in Malawi, *Why Father Why*, which focuses on the plight of a young boy who grows up without a father. The boy struggles through life and eventually makes a success of himself as a best-selling author, but he has suffered so many torments and deprivations along the way that he resolves to track down his father and ask him why he absconded, leaving the woman he impregnated and her unborn child to fend for themselves. When the feckless father fails to offer a satisfactory answer, the young man, by now a fabulously wealthy author, turns away from him and refuses to shelter, comfort and protect him in his old age. The heartless, deserting parent thereby gets his just deserts.

George, the boy hero, unlike most of Kalitera's other male protagonists, is a model of virtue who remains completely celibate before marriage. He won't even sleep with Mag, his fiancée, for fear of getting her pregnant. When another man seduces, impregnates and marries Mag, George tries to forget her, but a few years later, after the husband drives her and her child out of the house, George comes to Mag's rescue by marrying her and acting as surrogate father to her fatherless son. A complicating factor is that by this time he is engaged to marry Sue, a woman he loves equally deeply. When he tries to shed her, Sue, distraught, is seduced and impregnated by a married man who refuses to assume any responsibility for her and the unborn child. George, touched by her plight, comes to the rescue again by taking her as his second wife. The book concludes with a lengthy argument in favor of polygamy as the best solution to an age-old problem:

> Before the white man came our people married more than one wife. No matter who'll argue to the contrary, I will stand by my word that when it came to protecting girls and children, that system was the best ever.
>
> In those communities there were no mothers without husbands. No children without fathers. If you wanted a girl you simply married her regardless of the number of wives you had already. You didn't use her then discard her. This guaranteed that there was a responsible father to every pregnancy.
>
> If a husband died, his wife or wives immediately became the wife or wives of his brother or brothers. And this guaranteed that there would never be mothers without husbands. No children without fathers...
>
> This one-husband-one-wife system we've inherited from the white man...was ill-conceived. One had to agree that the idea was beautiful. One man worrying with no more than one woman and the children by her. But which one man was so holy that he ignored every other woman the moment he got married? The idea ignored

the maxim, "Boys will be boys." That was the reason it was a washout. Because everything which ignores human nature always failed...

In a nutshell what the west told us was "Don't bother with marrying more than one wife. What you should do is to marry one woman. Anybody. Now, if at any time you come across another woman you can't resist go ahead and have an affair with her. Use her as much as you like. And once you feel you've had enough of her, discard her..."

If you look at it that way, you will see that this system of one man one wife adopted from the west is the mother of so much suffering because it says that mothers without husbands are a normal thing; so are fatherless children. Yes, they may look normal, but mothers without husbands and fatherless children are perpetually miserable. And in my book the polygamous system is superior to this hypocritical monogamous system. Because it eliminates the misery. (393-395)

This frank and forceful argument may have been one of the factors that led to the commercial success of *Why Father Why*. According to Kalitera, the book was very popular, selling

possibly ten times more than any of the others. *Why Father Why* broke all the records. This is an everyday story, especially here. We've got fathers running away to the mines and leaving children unsupported. So there were many people, especially office girls, who came and said, "I want that book. I want to send it to George in Britain." (Kalitera 10)

Since Power Pen Books were marketed mainly in office buildings in Blantyre and other Malawian cities, Kalitera wrote about matters of immediate interest to secretaries, managers, businessmen and other white-collar workers. Many of his heroes and heroines are employed in offices of one sort or another, urban workplaces in which bureaucratic intrigues, dishonest business dealings, and behind-the-door intimacies between bosses and clerical staff are routine events.

Sometimes these office imbroglios serve merely as starting points for stories that carry the reader to rural or exotic environments: forests, farms, mines, airplanes, fishing boats. *To Ndirande Mountain with Love* begins as a fairly predictable account of an illicit love affair between a company publicity manager and his new secretary but quickly develops into a mountain adventure tale involving rape, kidnapping, attempted murder, hot pursuit, and exquisite revenge. *Why Son Why* and *Daughter Why Daughter* focus on urbanized, westernized individuals who, after a series of mishaps, become aware of the importance of establishing a family homestead on the land. Kalitera's villains ordinarily end up broken and in the red; his heroes and heroines, on the other hand, frequently wind up in the pink, having inherited vast riches, built up very solid business enterprises, married into money, or enjoyed windfalls such as winning first prize in a lottery. Virtue seldom is solely its own reward: a pot of gold usually accompanies it.

Most of Kalitera's stories are first-person narratives told in a brisk, colloquial idiom that is refreshingly direct. There are no ambiguities or purple passages, no strainings after novel or precious effects. Clear communication is the top priority. Stories often open with a gripping statement calculated to pique the reader's interest:

> Well, it is over, thank God. People, who include my friends and my wife, ask me if I could do it again. They could be teasing me and they could not be teasing me. Still they don't seem to understand that I can't be sure. and how can I be sure? Suppose my next secretary was even more beautiful than Memory? (*To Ndirande Mountain with Love* 9)

> I first suspected that Felix was fooling with Raymond's wife, Alice, almost 24 hours before I made up my mind that I was right. (*To Felix with Love* 9)

Maybe if it wasn't for the sake of the funeral Robert Kandulu would not have met the South African suitor of his daughter that day. (*Daughter Why Daughter* 9)

One fine afternoon some twenty-five years ago now a man was fatally stabbed by a hired assassin. (*Mother Why Mother* 9)

If Celia Zedi had dropped the baby face down in the pit toilet, she would have managed the killing she failed. (*She Died in My Bed* 132)

Kalitera then proceeds to build up suspense by involving the reader in a mystery or problem confronting the narrator/ protagonist. Often we are told right from the start what is most worrisome or vexing about the situation, but sometimes information is withheld to deepen the enigma, forcing us to empathize with a character who must take a crucial decision without being able to anticipate its eventual consequences. Kalitera is adept at putting us in a character's mind so that we can share his or her anxieties and obsessions. In one story, "On Wedding's Eve," he even allows us to penetrate the psychology of an angry water snake. In his best-told tales—*Why Father Why* and *To Ndirande Mountain with Love*, for instance—he succeeds in sustaining suspense to the very last chapter, thereby building to an effective climax.

Other appealing aspects of Kalitera's writing are its genial tone, lively sense of humor, and occasional flashes of what seems to be self-revelation. Kalitera evidently takes great pleasure in writing and in being known as a successful writer. Since all his narrators are presented as if writing their own story, and since several of them are said to have taken up writing as a career, it is amusing to note their remarks on the craft of writing, for one suspects that some of these may reflect Kalitera's views on his own profession. At one point in *A Taste of Business*, for instance, the narrator states:

But how on earth did one construct sentences that would carry a listener over every step you had taken, over all the things you had heard, over every beat your heart had missed in your desperation? How? I had read somewhere that accomplished writers often had the same dread. To put into words that clear picture they had in their mind! So that in the end their words would clearly and easily draw the same picture in the minds of the reader.

I am adding this piece about writers to try to slam into you the full picture of my frustration. Because if you understand that, if I had been a practised writer, my problem couldn't have been simpler, you will understand that as an ordinary man with an ordinary command of language my problem couldn't have been more difficult. (82)

And in *Why Father Why*, George, the would-be best-selling novelist, reflects:

The first time I had made up my mind that I wanted to be nothing but a writer, I had been horrified myself. I personally knew nobody who had become a writer. On the other hand I wanted two things in life. Money and fame. Not money alone. (258)

As every honest writer will admit it, what all writers want is to be applauded. So after producing my first piece of writing, I took it to Sue for criticism. I wanted to be told that I was better than Ian Fleming, Hammond Innes, James Hadley Chase, Erle Stanley Gardner, all bundled together.

Instead Sue told me, "I don't know how people become writers. But if they all begin this way, then you are a long way off. Why don't you go ahead and write to a correspondence school like you said you would?"

I could not help wondering if Mag would have said the same thing. But I took Sue's advice. Despite the pain. The next day I wrote to a school whose advertisement—in a magazine—had barked at me two weeks before: WE WANT PEOPLE WHO LOVE TO WRITE. (264-265)

When I become a writer, there are things I would like to say. And I am going to write solely for fellow Africans. (267)

Now, those who know how hard it is to fill a page with valuable writing will wonder how I could take ten pages at a sitting. You know what, it is so funny. A good writer will always find if very hard to fill a single page. A bad writer will always find it easy. (288)

Also, one of the characters in *Why Son Why* makes this comment on a leading journalist:

You see, Jack is a communicator. One of the greatest. There is very little about himself or the next man he doesn't want to lay bare. I guess that is what makes his writing stand out. Every piece of his writing is a revelation. I caught someone at one of the hotels the other day telling his friends, "Gentlemen, we've got to admit that Jack Kathumba has a wonderful brain. Here is what I mean. On page 241 in *No Oh No*, a woman tells a man that if he came into this world to receive, then even if he lived to be a hundred, he wasn't ever going to achieve anything. Because on earth, whatever may be the case elsewhere, people only succeed when they are giving and not getting. When I read that first time I told myself that Kathumba was mad. Then I read it a second and third time. That was when I realised that the man has something upstairs."*

Kalitera adds the asterisk to draw our attention to a footnote at the bottom of the page that reads:

*Something about giving, but not in these words was said in *Mother Why Mother* by Aubrey Kalitera. Published by Power Pen Books. (139-140)

In addition, there is a blurb on the back cover of this book where Kalitera quotes himself even more overtly:

Aubrey Kalitera himself says, "I have got my problems on earth. But none of them is on how to write well."

After reading a good sample of the fiction produced by this prolific, self-taught author, publisher, salesman and promoter of Malawian popular literature, the average reader is likely to agree with this boastful statement. And for those who might feel inclined to dispute it, Aubrey Kalitera, businessman *par excellence*, has the cold, hard sales figures to prove it true.

Dennis Brutus, Texas Poet

I first met Dennis Brutus in Los Angeles in March of 1967. I was a doctoral student at UCLA then, and Dennis was on his first major speaking tour in the United States, having made his way into exile in England after gaining release from prison and house arrest in South Africa just a year earlier. In Britain he had become active in a number of London-based anti-apartheid organizations, and if I remember correctly, it was his involvement in the campaign to exclude South Africa from the 1968 Olympics in Mexico City that occasioned his visit to North America. He was traveling as President of the South African Non-Racial Olympic Committee (SANROC), an organization he had founded in South Africa, and he was making his rounds to strategic points in the Western Hemisphere in an effort to marshal support for an international boycott of South African sports teams.

In those days Dennis was better known as a political activist than as a poet. After all, up to that point he had published only one slim volume of poems, *Sirens, Knuckles, Boots*, which had been issued in 1963 by the Mbari Centre in Nigeria and consequently was not widely available in the rest of the English-speaking world. However, his second volume, *Letters to Martha and Other Poems from a South African Prison*, was about to appear in Heinemann's ubiquitous African Writers Series the following year, and this, more than any other single publication, was to make him more conspicuous to the reading public. The fact that both these books were banned in South Africa added further interest and notoriety to his verse, especially his prison poems, so his literary career was about to take off in a major way, even though he was doing nothing strenuous to promote it. Instead, he was devoting all his energy to the sports campaign; poetry was only a sideline, an avocation, something one might do to fill up spare moments at a bus stop or in an airport waiting room. Then, as now, he never put poetry first.

Dennis gave a talk at UCLA and read a few of his poems, and afterwards John Povey and I sought him out in his hotel room in order to tape-record an interview with him. John and I were more interested in eliciting his views on poetry than on politics, but the discussion ranged widely over a variety of topics, on all of which Dennis expressed himself with great clarity and conviction. I recall having been impressed not only with his facility for articulating ideas but also with his friendliness and relaxed unpretentiousness. He was very approachable and seemed to relish engaging conversation.

The next time I saw Dennis was in the summer of 1969 at the Pan-African Cultural Festival in Algiers, where he was part of a South African delegation that included Alex La Guma, Mazisi Kunene, and Cosmo Pieterse. Again he was quite accessible and approachable, and between sessions at the conference and cultural events in the city, we had a number of chats about literary matters, chats that were continued at greater length a few weeks later in London as I was on my way back to the United States. Although he had lived there for only a few years, Dennis already knew his way around London like a veteran cab-driver, and as we moved about the city, he pointed out numerous landmarks and monuments, filling me in on details of their history. He was an excellent tour guide, and I learned a great deal about London and about Dennis himself on that brief visit.

In the fall of 1969 I began teaching at the University of Texas at Austin, which had just established an African and Afro-American Research Institute to promote and publish research in Black Studies. One of my responsibilities was to found and edit a new biannual journal, *Research in African Literatures*, which was to be distributed to interested individuals and institutions free of charge. At my suggestion the Institute also launched an

Occasional Publications Series to bring out pamphlet-length contributions by distinguished visitors to our campus. Like the journal, these booklets were to be sent out gratis to everyone on our subscription list and to anyone else who requested them. In those good old days, Texas oil money was gushing into the university, permitting a major expansion of facilities and programs. With such support, there was no need to charge subscription fees for new publications or to worry about such irrelevancies as cost-effectiveness. The Research Institute was meant to generate and disseminate research, and this it could do best by simply giving publications away. The first issues of *Research in African Literatures* and the first two Occasional Publications appeared in 1970 and were mailed to about two thousand libraries and scholars throughout the world.

Dennis made singular contributions to both series. In the third issue of *Research in African Literatures* (Vol. 2, No. 1) he offered a memorial tribute to the late Arthur Nortje, a South African poet who had once been his high school student in Port Elizabeth. To the Occasional Publications Series he contributed *Poems from Algiers*, a collection of nine pensive poems written while he was attending the Pan-African Cultural Festival. This pamphlet included seven pages of his own comments on the poems as well. Everything—poems, comments, table of contents, title page—was written in his own distinctive calligraphic hand.

This was Brutus's third book of poetry, and though in form and style the individual poems in it more closely resembled the plain, laconic verse in *Letters to Martha* than the ornate, knotted, cerebral poetry in *Sirens, Knuckles, Boots*, there was also greater complexity in certain of the Algiers poems than could be found in much of what he had written based on his prison experiences. *Poems from Algiers* therefore represented a new turn in Brutus's poetry that came close to being a synthesis between his earliest intense poeticizing and his moody, colloquial musings in jail. Certainly this small collection offered some fine examples of qualities that grew to be typical of Brutus's early exile verse: a special sensitivity to place and circumstance, a plaintive nostalgia for South Africa, a brooding awareness of restlessness and tension underlying surface calm.

What justified the inclusion of Dennis's poetry in the Occasional Publications Series was his visit to the University of Texas at Austin in February 1970. He was back in the United States doing a stint of substitute-teaching for Es'kia Mphahlele at the University of Denver then, so we invited him to come to Austin to participate in a campus colloquium on "The Black Experience." Of course, while he was in town, we put him to work in a number of other ways too: he gave a public lecture, a press conference, a television interview, and met with student groups to answer questions about South Africa. On top of all this, he agreed to visit an African literature class that had been reading his poetry and wanted to know more about his life and art; a partial transcript of his illuminating dialogue with that class was published in the African and Afro-American Research Institute's third Occasional Publication, *Palaver: Interviews with Five African Writers in Texas*, which appeared in 1972 (Lindfors). That transcript still makes interesting reading today, for it contains some of Dennis's most extensive explications of his own verse as well as his thoughtful justification for switching from a complex to a simple poetic idiom.

In the summer of 1970 I was back in Europe to attend a congress of the International Comparative Literature Association held in Bordeaux, and I stopped by London again to visit libraries and bookshops as well as to see Dennis. While he had been in Austin in February, I had shown him the university's Humanities Research Center (HRC), an archive of rare books and manuscripts that had been established by Harry Ransom, an ex-president of the university who was then serving as Chancellor of the University of Texas System. The HRC, which had been one of the pioneers in the acquisition of twentieth-century literary manuscripts, had some South African holdings of interest, among them a large collection of letters by Olive Schreiner, a complete file of the papers of H.C. Bosman, some holograph poems and letters by Roy Campbell, the typescript of one of Nadine

Gordimer's novels, and even some materials in Afrikaans by Uys Krige. But it held nothing by "non-white" South African authors, and it had made no effort to collect papers from writers in other parts of Africa. I felt that it would be a good idea to encourage the HRC to take an interest in acquiring literary manuscripts from these neglected writers, particularly from those in exile whose papers might otherwise never be preserved. I had sounded Dennis out on this to see if he had any manuscripts that he would be willing to allow the HRC to consider adding to its South African holdings. Although he had seldom kept the drafts of his poems, he thought that some of his early notebooks and holograph love lyrics might still be in the possession of friends in South Africa to whom he had sent them years ago, but given his status as a banned person in South Africa, it might be dangerous or risky for those friends if he now tried to retrieve such papers. However, he thought he might have in London a quantity of the working drafts of what he had written since leaving South Africa, and I would be welcome to collect these whenever I next passed through England. I took Dennis up on this that summer and carried back to Austin several cartons of his papers which I promptly wheeled over to the campus administration building and deposited in the suite of offices occupied by Chancellor Harry Ransom.

Dennis's papers were a fascinating amalgam of scraps, scripts and cuttings. He had a habit of writing poems whenever the mood struck him, putting them down on whatever paper was within easy reach. So there were verses penned or pencilled on the backs of envelopes, on the pages of newspapers, on magazine covers, on restaurant menus, on departmental memos, on pieces of junk mail, on laundry slips, on scorecards, even on airline vomit bags. In some cases one couldn't tell if a particular scribbling was intended to be a poem, a terse message, a test of his writing instrument, a reminder to himself, or merely an off-the-cuff remark or reflective rumination. One example I remember with some amusement consisted of the following haiku-like lines:

Dungbeetles in Texas
work
awfully hard.

Was this a poem, an entymological observation, a comment about me, a jibe at the eccentric exertions of the HRC, or all of the above? Like some of Brutus's most economical verse, these verbally frugal lines were open to a multitude of interpretations and perhaps were meant to be so. On the other hand, it is entirely possible that they were nothing more than a fleeting thought mindlessly captured in ink, a genuine jot of ephemera.

The manuscripts sat in Chancellor Ransom's office for well over a year and no action was ever taken on them. I don't know if Ransom ever found time to look at them, or whether his scrutiny of them would have made any difference. Ransom himself was at that time being eased out of administrative work—being "kicked upstairs" was the language often used to describe the process—and given a sinecure as official historian of the university, but he died before he could complete the book that was to be his last academic assignment. In the meantime control of the HRC had passed into other hands, and the new regime remained complacently indifferent to African acquisitions. Eventually I wheeled the boxes back to my office and posted them on to Dennis, who was by then teaching at Northwestern University. The manuscripts subsequently were purchased by Northwestern's Melville J. Herskovits Africana Library, which later, with Dennis's assistance, went on to acquire some important papers of the late Arthur Nortje.

Nonetheless, one good thing did come out of the sequestration of Dennis's boxes in Texas. In our discussions in London Dennis and I had hatched a plan to subvert South African censorship laws by publishing a booklet of his verse under a pseudonym and funneling copies of this publication to South African bookshops, libraries and literary media. We thought this would be a fine prank to play on the Censorship Board, so we set about creating our own publishing house, Troubadour Press, the total plant and property of which consisted of a small post office box in Del Valle, Texas, a community just outside Austin. The wheels of production at Troubadour Press turned rapidly, and lo and behold, before the end of 1970, we had churned out our first and only publication: *Thoughts Abroad*, a 28-page collection of poems by "John Bruin." The blurb on the back cover stated that

> John Bruin is a South African currently teaching and writing outside his country. He is, as his work shows, both widely traveled and homesick. He has already been published in many magazines, in various countries and languages, and has a steadily growing reputation as perhaps one of the first South African poets to achieve international recognition. Two books of his poetry are due to appear shortly; for fuller information write to Troubadour Press.

The booklet had a striking cover—a modernistic sketch of an agonized thinker drawn by the South African artist-in-exile Feni Dumile, whose name was disguised in the credit line as Fanie du Mealie Bruin.

There were other harmless jokes in the publicity materials we disseminated. Pretending that Troubadour Press was a thriving publishing enterprise, we prepared a flier listing a dozen additional titles that were about to be released, but to avoid any possibility of mail fraud, we took care to instruct recipients of the flier to order and pay for only those books that were already in print—in other words, only John Bruin's *Thoughts Abroad*. The other books on the list had covertly humorous titles, the hilarity of which would have been understood and appreciated by only a handful of friends, family members, or faculty in the College of Liberal Arts at the University of Texas at Austin, none of whom received the fliers. Our mailings went exclusively to bookshops, university libraries and literary magazines in South Africa and to a few African Studies libraries in the United States. And to keep within the letter of the law, we submitted two copies of the booklet to the Library of Congress so it could be copyrighted in the name of Troubadour Press.

To add to the fun, I wrote a poker-faced appraisal of the poetry of John Bruin for *Africa Today* in which I expressed great admiration for this enigmatic, peripatetic poet whose intriguing volume of verse had unexpectedly turned up in a local bookshop. This wasn't the only assessment of Bruin's oeuvre to appear in print. One of my doctoral students, Barney McCartney, wrote an excellent review of *Thoughts Abroad* for *Ufahamu* without being in the least aware that the author whose poetry he was commenting on was really Dennis Brutus. And Nadine Gordimer, contacted and let into the secret while she was on a speaking tour in the United States, agreed to review the book for *South African Outlook*, even though she could have faced serious penalties back home had it been discovered that she was discussing a banned author.

This modest effort at publicity yielded modest dividends, generating a few sales in South Africa and a few in the United States, but we disposed of most of the one thousand copies in the print run by sending them directly to Dennis's friends, acquaintances and former colleagues in South Africa. We had no interest in making Troubadour Press a going concern. The company had been created solely as a front for flouting one of the great idiocies of the South African legal code: the censorship of poetry.

But although the book was in essence a private joke, the poems in it were actually rather good. Dennis, in assembling his papers for the HRC, had gathered together verses he had written in various parts of the world—London, Bristol, Belfast, Stockholm, Paris, Grenoble, Rome, Frankfurt, Dubrovnik, Cairo, Algiers, Mbabane, Tehran, New Delhi, Sydney, Nandi, New York, etc.—and then left me to select the final 28 and to organize them into a coherent sequence. In this wide-ranging collection some of the rhetorical strategies from *Sirens, Knuckles, Boots* were again in evidence, especially the confessional voice of a poet-speaker who complains of being "the slave of an habituated love" for his homeland/mistress. There was also more careful attention paid to stanza structure, wordplay, and rounded framing devices than was the case in most of Dennis's prison poems. But as in *Poems from Algiers*, which had been published only a few days earlier, the mood throughout *Thoughts Abroad* was one of homesick reverie. The exiled poet was now at liberty to wander the world, but no matter where he went, his thoughts kept returning to his native land. In that sense, he was not, and never would be, completely free while he was abroad. These morose poetic thoughts later achieved wider circulation when they were integrated into Brutus's next major volume, *A Simple Lust*, which was published in the Heinemann African Writers Series in 1973.

During the 1972-73 academic year I was away in Nigeria doing research, but Dennis and I kept in regular touch, for I needed his help in checking the transcript of a lengthy series of interviews I had conducted with him in London. A portion of this transcript, with questions edited out so it appears to be an autobiographical statement rather than an interview, was published in the first issue of *The Benin Review*, a new Nigerian literary journal founded by Abiola Irele.

When I returned to Texas the following year, I learned that Dennis was beginning to feel a little restless at Northwestern and was ready for a change of scene, preferably to a warmer climate. With support from the English Department and the African and Afro-American Studies Program at the University of Texas at Austin, it was possible to arrange a Visiting Professorship for him in English and Ethnic Studies, and he came down to Austin for the 1974-75 academic year. This proved to be propitious timing, for it was at the African Studies Association conference in Chicago in the fall of 1974 that a small group of scholars met to discuss the possibility of forming an African Literature Association. Nearly all concerned felt that such an organization was needed, and it was agreed that an inaugural conference should be held in Austin in March of 1975 to launch it. Dennis and I had traveled up to Chicago with other Texas faculty (Hal Wylie, Ed Steinhart, Carolyn Parker) and graduate students (Wayne Kamin, Barney McCartney) in my VW bus, and on the return trip the bunch of us began laying plans for the conference.

The University of Texas could not provide funds to support a meeting of a professional association, so we asked the Dean of Liberal Arts and the Dean of General and Comparative Studies to underwrite the expenses of a separate Symposium which would draw colleagues from around the country and abroad who could participate in a business meeting afterwards and go through the formalities necessary to establish a new international scholarly body devoted to the study and teaching of African literatures. The Symposium would focus on contemporary South African literature, and our plan was to invite South African writers to give keynote addresses and then have writers from other parts of Africa respond to the issues raised. We did not have sufficient funds to fly in anyone all the way from Africa, so we had to rely on bringing to Austin only those writers who were then somewhere in the United States. Fortunately, there was an abundance of talent available. The keynote speakers were Es'kia Mphahlele, Mongane Wally Serote, Oswald Mtshali, Keorapetse Kgositsile, Cosmo Pieterse, Mazisi Kunene, Dan Kunene, and of course Brutus himself; included among the respondents were Chinua Achebe, Kofi Awoonor, Ama Ata Aidoo, Ali Mazrui, Peter Nazareth, Pol Ndu, Emmanuel Obiechina, Romanus Egudu, and Biodun Jeyifo. Never before had such a constellation of African literary stars assembled in one place in the United States. The Symposium events drew large audiences, and when the ALA was formally inaugurated, more than four hundred writers, scholars, students and townspeople signed on as members.

The success of this Symposium and the birth and baptism of the ALA owed a great deal to the organizational skills of Dennis Brutus. He was the one who formed an efficient Austin Working Committee to oversee local arrangements, he was the one who persuaded the writers to come, he was the one who ran the business meeting at the end of it all that resulted in the creation of a viable and vigorous ALA. Appropriately enough, he was also the one elected by acclamation to serve as the ALA's first Chairperson.

The Symposium-cum-Conference afforded an occasion for more Occasional Publications. Registrants at Austin received in their conference packets two booklets of poetry: *South African Voices*, which featured contributions by the seven poets participating in the Symposium, and *China Poems* by Dennis Brutus. The latter was a by-product of Dennis's visit in August-September of 1973 to the People's Republic of China where, as Vice-President of the South African Table Tennis Board, he was invited to witness a Friendship International Table Tennis Tournament. He had started reading translations of Mao Tse-tung's poetry shortly before undertaking this journey, and his "China Poems" were efforts at simulating in English the kind of lucid compression found in certain Oriental forms of verse. As he put it in the explanatory notes appended to the poems,

> The trick is to say little (the nearer to nothing, the better) and to suggest much—as much as possible. The weight of meaning hovers around the words (which should be as flat as possible) or is brought by the reader/hearer. Non-emotive, near-neutral sounds should generate unlimited resonances in the mind; the delight is in the tight-rope balance between saying very little and implying a great deal. (35)

Although Brutus had occasionally experimented with very brief forms earlier in his career, these "China Poems" gave an entirely new slant to his work; he was now swinging away from the gently stylized stanzas of his early exile verse to a more rigorous and disciplined economy of statement. Some poems consisted of just three words! Even the booklet itself was designed to be a syncretic product, part Western, part Chinese, but all blended together harmoniously. As in *Poems from Algiers*, these tersest of verses were reproduced in Dennis's attractive calligraphic script, but in addition there were beautifully drawn

Chinese translations specially prepared by Ko Ching-Po, one of the translators of Mao's poetry.

There was another little booklet of Dennis's poetry made available at the Symposium too, this one published under the revived imprint of Troubadour Press (now operating out of a post office box in Austin) and edited by Wayne Kamin and Chip Dameron, graduate students in the English Department at the University of Texas at Austin. Entitled *Strains*, this booklet carried samples of Dennis's output from September 1962 to February 1975 and therefore was written in a variety of poetic styles. Some of the poems had appeared earlier in various magazines and journals, and others were scraps gleaned from Dennis's unpublished papers. Kamin and Dameron had sifted through the typescripts that had been prepared from everything resembling poetry in the boxes of papers that had been stored temporarily in Chancellor Ransom's office, and had made judicious selections from these remnants as well as from fresh manuscripts that Dennis had supplied them. Dennis himself was to employ the same collage technique in his next major collection, *Stubborn Hope*, which was comprised of some of the same miscellaneous bits and pieces composed at different stages of his career. Both volumes are interesting as diachronic synopses of Brutus's poetic interests and proclivities. One finds a whole smorgasbord of variegated treats in each.

Dennis sometimes wrote poems about Texas and Texans, but this is not what makes it possible to call him a Texas poet. Rather, it was those four little booklets of poetry published deep in the heart of Central Texas between 1970 and 1975 that give the Lone Star State the privilege of claiming him as one of its local products. He may not be from this place, he may no longer be in this place, and he may never have contemplated any permanent attachment to this place, but because some of his poetry first made its way into indelible print here, he left an enduring mark on this place and therefore will always be regarded by Texans not as a stranger or a visitor or an exile, but as a true native Texan.

So we carve structures,
so we leave striations in the rocks. (Bruin 10)

Wordplay

Perverted Proverbs in Onitsha Chapbooks

One of the many tragic consequences of Nigeria's civil war was the destruction of Onitsha, a thriving commercial city on the Niger River. Besides having been the largest urban center in the Eastern Region of the country and a hub of Igbo economic activity, Onitsha was the home of a vigorous small press publishing industry which catered to the reading tastes of Nigeria's newly literate English-speaking proletariat. For twenty years a dozen or more local printers and publishers had mass-produced inexpensive pamphlet novels, courtesy books, courtship manuals, political biographies, histories, educational aids, and books of moral instruction and practical advice for Nigerian city dwellers. A few of these chapbooks were written by university graduates and internationally known Nigerian authors (e.g., Chinua Achebe, Cyprian Ekwensi), but most were turned out by writers with no formal education beyond high school or, in some cases, elementary school. They were avidly read by hundreds of students, clerks, traders, craftsmen, taxi drivers and other semi-educated townsfolk who wanted to practice the language they had learned at school. Unlike the London-published novels and plays authored by the educated elite, the chapbooks were truly a literature of the people, by the people and for the people.

A few representative titles will reveal something of the character of this popular literature. Many of the chapbooks are novelettes or plays dealing with love problems in the city:

Saturday Night Disappointment
Florence in the River of Temptation
Disaster in the Realms of Love
Miss Cordelia in the Romance of Destiny
Mabel the Sweet Honey that Poured Away
The True Confessions of "Folake"
Rose Only Loved My Money
My Seven Daughters are after Young Boys
How a Passenger Collector Posed and Got a Lady Teacher in Love

There are also fictionalized biographies and plays honoring outstanding political leaders:

Dr. Nkrumah in the Struggle for Freedom
How Lumumba Suffered in Life and Died in Katanga
The Life Story and Death of John Kennedy
The Statements of Hitler before the World War
The Trials of Lumumba, Jomo Kenyatta and St. Paul

In addition to fictional works there are many chapbooks which are factual or at least pretend to be so. These are usually meant to educate or improve the reader in a variety of ways:

How to Write Good English and Compositions
How to Write Love Letters, Toasts and Business Letters
The Way to Get Money: The Best Wonderful Book for Money Mongers
One Hundred Popular Facts about "Sex and Facts"
How to Live Bachelor's Life and Girl's Life without Much Mistakes
How to Marry a Good Girl and Live in Peace with Her

Then too there are moral and didactic treatises which attempt to alert the unwary to the perils of urban life:

Beware of Harlots and Many Friends: The World is Hard
Money Hard to Get but Easy to Spend
No Money, Much Expenses, Enemies and Bad Friends Kill a Man
Trust No-body in Time Because Human Being is Trickish and Difficult

Life Turns Man Up and Down: Money and Girls Turn Man Up and Down

As can be seen from these titles, Onitsha chapbooks provide a wealth of useful data for anthropologists, sociologists, political scientists, psychologists and historians interested in the preoccupations of the common man in contemporary Africa. They also yield information of importance to literary analysts, linguists, aestheticians, and folklorists who would rather study verbal behavior than social attitudes. Like oxen in an Augean stable, the chapbooks furnish an almost inexhaustible supply of raw material for energetic scholars to work on.

One of the most interesting phenomena to observe in the chapbooks is the transmission of fixed-phrase folklore. What happens to common English proverbs, idioms and figures of speech when they are used by Nigerians with an imperfect command of the English language? If they change, how do they change? What kinds of mutation occur? Do these new or perverted forms make any sense? What, in short, can we learn from such material about the cross-cultural transmission of folklore? We shall attempt to answer these questions using data collected from roughly 75 Onitsha chapbooks.

Before beginning, it is necessary to state that Nigerian chapbook writers tend to be very adventurous in their use of English. They do not hesitate to coin new words or to rush in where conservative grammarians fear to tread. Some are addicted to polysyllables and bombast, others to lurid purple prose. It is not unusual, for example, to find sentences such as these:

The following day was greatly terrible.
Her countenance showed such of infuriation owing to enviousness.
Our love has agility, incombustility, and civility. It is irreproachable,
    unblushable and irrevocable.
Severe and solemn tears ran down the rails of his cheeks.
They squalled, embraced and fell into a mighty abyss of love
    making.

> In a fiery rejoinder to their love protestations I gave them a very
>   cold shoulder.
> It was the highest eccentric subtle, ever experienced.

Chapbook writers, by this kind of linguistic audacity, sometimes
achieve strikingly original effects, but it is not always easy to tell
when these effects are intentional and when purely accidental.
In examining perverted forms of fixed-phrase folklore we must
be alert to the possibility of deliberate distortion, even when the
distortion seems nonsensical or noncommunicative.

Another factor complicating analysis of these materials is the
high incidence of printing errors. Some of the compositors who
set type for chapbook publishers have very little training or
professional experience and less formal schooling than the
authors themselves. They are apt to make several spelling
mistakes on every page. Occasionally these mistakes give tired
clichés an illicit new life:

> Love is a worm affection.
> Stella could not give the least room for other women to warm their
>   way into Bob's affection.
> ...a bird of roses.
> ...a means of lovelihood.
> ...a ball in a China shop.
> ...head over feels in love.

One may assume that the following proverbs were
unintentionally altered by unskillful typesetters:

> A rolling stone gathers no morse.
> I am too old a bird to be caught with charfs.
> All that gilters is not gold.
> If wishers were hoses beggars might ride.
> Never buy a pity in a poke.

But occasionally one finds minimally altered proverbs which
make perfectly good sense in their altered form:

Do not rub Peter to pay Paul.
Empty vassels make the most sound.
A leopard cannot change his sports.
East and West name is best.

In such cases it may be difficult to determine whether the proverb has been misprinted or misconstrued and whether the mistake is the author's or the typesetter's. In novelettes and plays, of course, the context in which the proverb is quoted provides a good clue, but one has no help at all with the context-free proverbs recorded in books like J. Abiakam's *49 Wise Sayings, 72 Idioms, 44 Questions & Answers and Some Speeches of World Leaders Past and Present,* or N.O. Njoku's *Teach Your-self Proverbs, Idioms, Wise Sayings, Laws, Rights of a Citizen, English Applications and Many Other Things for Schools and Colleges,* or Charles N. Eze's *Learn to Speak 360 Interesting Proverbs and Know Your True Brother.* In jungles like these, the explorer must watch his step.

After allowing for such difficulties, however, it is possible to identify at least five different processes of change which affect fixed-phrase folklore in the chapbooks. These are Addition, Deletion, Substitution, Rearrangement, and Transformation. By Addition is meant any change which augments the original without greatly modifying its meaning or syntactic structure. The simplest form of Addition is the alteration of a singular to a plural. For example, several chapbook authors speak of paying traitors back "in their own coins." A man who becomes the favorite of a woman is sometimes described as "the apple of her eyes." One also finds pluralized proverbs such as "Birds of the same feathers flock together." Of course, Addition can mean added words too, as in "Blood is factually thicker than water" and "he kicked off the bucket." Longer examples of Addition can be found in three versions of a single proverb: "Call a spade a spade and nothing but a spade"; "Let us call a spade a spade and not a fork"; "As a woman, it should not be in my power to call a spade a spade in this particular affair but all right thinking citizens can understand me if I call it a knife." Here the idea of calling a spade a spade (i.e., speaking frankly and honestly) is not substantially changed by the extra verbiage. Meaning and structure remain virtually intact.

Deletion may be defined as the opposite of Addition—that is, any change which diminishes the original without greatly modifying its meaning of syntactic structure. Deletions tend to be infrequent in Nigerian chapbooks. One finds statements such as "Why should we continue to swallow his pronouncements, hook and sinker?" and "between the devil and the deep sea," but more significant omissions are lacking. The tendency to add details is stronger than the tendency to subtract.

Substitution, the replacement of one word or set of words with another, is more common than both Addition and Deletion. Any part of speech—noun, verb, adjective, adverb, preposition, etc.—in a proverb or idiom may undergo Substitution, but the underlying meaning of the statement will not change appreciably. For example, one finds expressions such as "the apple in his eyes," "the apple of my heart," "a lion under the skin of a sheep," "Cordelia has turned into a new leaf," "It is not wise for one to hook in troubled water," "A bird at hand is worth two in the bush," "Unsteady lies the head that wears a crown," "Nothing venture, nothing have," and "Nothing venture, nothing coin." The substitutions here are quite logical, indicating that the basic concepts have been grasped even though the expression of them is not perfectly traditional. There is also at least one example of the substitution of a homonym: "Do not carry coal to new castle." Such a substitution reveals that the proverb was not properly understood by the chapbook author, but the meaning which the new proverb communicates is not radically different from that of the original. Had the name of the city been Oldcastle, however, the homonymic substitution would have resulted in a significant difference in meaning. Another type of Substitution is the replacement of many words with synonyms: e.g., "Birds of identical plumage congregate in the same proximity." This is usually done deliberately to achieve a comic effect. More common are the proverbs which are altered by a double process of

Substitution and Addition, typical examples being "When the cat is away from the house then the rat governs," "Everybody is made of mud no matter your colour, and to mud must everybody go," "Those who never give their children the rod must not wonder if their children become a rod to them." Again, no matter how far the new version departs from the original, the basic core of meaning remains unchanged.

Rearrangement, the fourth process of fixed-phrase folklore perversion, may be defined as the restructuring of a statement without major additions, deletions or substitutions. "Swim or sink," "a tooth for a tooth and an eye for an eye," and "fell heals [sic] over head in love" are illustrations of one type of Rearrangement, the reversal of parallel items. "The hay is made while the sun shined [sic]" is an example of syntactic Rearrangement. Rearrangement is not a very common phenomenon in the chapbooks, but it occurs often enough to suggest that certain proverbs and idioms do not have a stable form in Nigeria.

Transformation, the fifth process, is the most important kind of alteration an item of folklore can undergo, for it involves a change of meaning as well as, in some cases, a change of structure. The simplest proverbial transformations in the chapbooks probably derive from mispronunciations or mishearings of English words. For instance, in "Once beaten twice shy" the crucial transformation is simply the substitution of one phoneme for another. This is also the case in the proverb "The taste of the puding [sic] is in the eating," but there is evidence that this particular perverted form is well known in Nigeria, for it appears, still further transformed, in another chapbook as "The sweetness of the food is in the tasting." Another possible example of auditory error is the misquotation of an almost proverbial line from Shakespeare's *Merchant of Venice*: "The quality of mercy is strange." There is no contextual evidence to suggest that this misquotation was deliberate. Like the proverbial transformations cited above, it appears to have been a blooper, albeit a meaningful one in the situation in which it was applied. Quite a few transformed proverbs bear a close resemblance to the parent proverb from which they spring, but they always differ somewhat in meaning. "If birds of like feather met they must be happy" is not too far away from the original, and "One can't eat his cake and have it back again" departs from the archetypal version only in its visceral imagery. Naturally, one must be very cautious in commenting on certain permutations because they may not be permutations at all. There is good evidence, for instance, that the seemingly garbled proverb "One is not sure of one's cake until one has taken it" descends directly from Igbo oral tradition.[1] It is not a perverted English proverb but a standard Igbo proverb translated into English. We must be alert to such analogues from indigenous sources.

Of the true perversions the most interesting are those in which the original message is turned inside out. "We must not cut our noses to make our faces fine" and "Dogs...will always back [sic] and what is worse, some of them will bite" are typical examples of proverbs which are made to mean just the opposite of what they usually mean. The chapbook author is not only in error; he is dead wrong.

It would be useful to know which English proverbs are consistently perverted by Nigerian chapbook writers and which are not, but a more comprehensive study of both the chapbooks and their authors is needed before such generalizations can be attempted. However, a few preliminary observations can now be made about how and why fixed-phrase folklore changes in the chapbooks. First, it should be stressed that except for a few major transformations the changes are minimal. Chapbook writers are more apt to add or substitute details which do not affect the meaning of a statement than they are to delete essential information. Also the form of the statement remains roughly the same; rearrangement of anything but parallel items is extremely rare. When transformations do occur, they appear to result from a misunderstanding of the original statement and a rationalization of the consequences. That is to say, the chapbook writers who fail to comprehend the meaning of a particular proverb will use it only after changing its wording so that it makes perfectly good sense. They are not likely to quote something that is complete gibberish to them. And when quoting fixed-phrase folklore that they know well and understand fully, they tend to be quite conservative. This study has dealt only with perverted forms. Many English proverbs and idioms, indeed the majority, are never mutilated or misused by chapbook authors. This fact, combined with the overwhelming evidence that fixed-phrase folklore transformations occur almost exclusively as a result of misunderstanding and subsequent rationalization, suggests that cross-cultural transmission of fixed-phrase folklore from native to non-native speakers of a given language proceeds smoothly, efficiently and without much cultural or linguistic static. Or as a chapbook writer might put it, "Monkey see, monkey do am just right, almost."[2]

---

[1] Cf. "A man could only be sure of what he had put away safely in his gut," a proverb used by Igbo novelist Chinua Achebe in *A Man of the People*. (167)

[2] For further information on Onitsha chapbooks, see Obiechina and Dodson as well as the bibliography prepared by Hogg and Sternberg.

All the News in Fits of Print: An Examination of Nigerian Newspaper Headlines

Reading a contemporary Nigerian newspaper is an experience akin to witnessing a cross-campus "streak."[1] One may be impressed with by the energy and enthusiasm that go into this kind of educational effort, or shocked by the unusual nature of some of the raw material prominently displayed, or amused by the absurdity of such eccentric exertions in pursuit of better public exposure of mundane human facts, or perhaps puzzled why so many insignificant, seemingly frivolous, private actions require so much coverage from day to day. One is tempted to ask, "Where is the end? How much longer will active citizens continue to bear it? When will the winds of change that are sweeping across the African continent bring blushes to the brazen newspaper columnist doing his daily strip? When, in brief, will such naked cheek be redressed? If standards are falling, if the moral mantle in which the nation was once wrapped is today being shucked off, if the unsensational, old-fashioned straitlaced coverall is now dropping to a new low, then surely the body politic is entitled to know why its most vital organs are being openly exercised in such a crude and uncouth manner. Why all the hustle-bustle? Why so much emphasis on racy, scandalous activities? What makes a newspaper run and run and run until it ultimately becomes run-down?"

In Nigeria the answer seems to be that every newspaper wants to earn a good track record by maintaining a winning streak. To do so, it must make money. In other words, it must sell well; there must be something in it every day that a tremendous number of Nigerians will want to read. One sure way of achieving this kind of mass appeal is to pander to the interests of the lowest common denominator in the reading audience. In order to survive without government subsidies, without becoming the mouthpiece of a political party or economic cabal, without relying upon "soft money" of one sort or another, newspapers in developing countries must strive to become truly popular media which speak to the entire literate populace.

This was not always the case. In Nigeria and other corners of the European colonial empire the first indigenous newspapers were intended for a tiny elite or educated class who had learned to read and needed printed texts on which to practice this newly acquired skill. Many of the early printing presses in Africa were set up by missionaries who published religious materials to reinforce the message they were teaching and preaching in mission schools. For instance, the first known newspaper in Nigeria, the *Iwe Irohin fun awon ara Egba Yorubas* (the newspaper for Egba people and the Yorubas), was established in 1859 primarily as a news bulletin for the Christian Missionary Society (CMS); as might be expected, it was edited by a European missionary, Rev. Henry Townsend, who had started putting the Yoruba language into written form eleven years earlier (Hachten 145). It has been estimated that by the time the maiden issue of *Iwe Irohin* appeared, three thousand Yorubas had learned to read their language. The first Bible in Yoruba was printed by the same press three years later. Obviously, the emphasis in this pioneer vernacular printing industry was on moral instruction, not immoral entertainment.

Newspapers soon began springing up like toadstools in the British West African colonies. By the turn of the century thirty-four had appeared in Sierra Leone, nineteen in the Gold Coast, nine in Nigeria and one in the Gambia—a total of sixty-three in all, but only a dozen of these lasted a decade or more (Hachten 145). Most were written in English and read both by British residents in West Africa and by those indigenes who had learned the colonial tongue. However, a good many were now edited not by missionaries but by educated Africans who had taken up newspaper publishing as a means of supplementing their income or disseminating their views (July 345-373). During this period journalism gradually grew into a respectable profession, especially in major urban centers which had a literate population large enough to sustain one or more newspapers. It was in certain of these papers that the first inklings of African nationalism were seen in print. Later, particularly from the mid-1930s until independence, newspapers tended to become platforms for nationalist agitation; quite a few were actually founded, owned and edited by leading politicians or major political parties. At the end of the pre-independence era, the primary function of the press was to politicize the masses, not to preach the word of a European god.

After independence, African newspapers found they needed a different orientation. There was still a lot of political news to report, but in some countries it came to be considered unpatriotic if not downright treasonable to criticize the government or the head of state. Official censorship was occasionally threatened or invoked to ensure that the public did not hear too much bad news about their leaders. The emphasis now—as in other shaky regimes throughout the world—was on good news. Also, the rapid expansion of primary and secondary education in most African countries had dramatically increased the size of the reading public in a fairly short period of time; there were suddenly many more people willing, able, and eager to buy newspapers. Competition for this vast new market led many newspapers to establish chains and to adopt tabloid tactics. Helen Kitchen reports that even before Nigeria became independent the London *Daily Mirror* had acquired the Lagos *Daily Times* and had transformed it into a racy periodical which managed to out-sell its nationalist rivals by sheer abundance of news and pictures and by avoiding anything which might "give color to the suspicion that it is playing journalistic stooge to the Imperial power" (77). Other papers followed suit; some succeeded by employing the same formula, others failed, but the loudest and splashiest inevitably seemed to last longest. The Nigerian press, having moved from the snow-white purity of missionary evangelism through the fiery crimson of nationalist fervor, ultimately turned yellow in response to popular demand.

In the 1970s the average Nigerian newspaper was a raucous rag preoccupied with sex, crime and local politics. One found some sober features on serious subjects but these were frequently all but obliterated by a tangled thicket of boldface headlines calling attention to more sensational matters. Rosalynde Ainslie's description of the Nigerian press in 1966 was still remarkably accurate:

> The stock-in-trade of Nigerian journalism is the human interest story, culled from the criminal courts or the latest scandal involving a public figure. Interpretation of the law of libel, as opposed to that of the sedition laws, seems to be liberal enough to permit personal attacks of a kind rarely met with in the British Press, or even in that of East Africa. And headlines are not designed to spare delicate sensibilities. Thus the *Daily Sketch*, the West Regional Government newspaper, is rich in headings such as: "Death for Akure Farmer—he laughs as judge shows him the way to the gallows." Its world news is largely confined to "Briefs," where "U.S. Jet Shot Down" and "India Joins Space Race" receive equal attention with a story on the breaking of a prostitution ring in St. Louis, U.S.A. Political and general interest features are usually syndicated stories from British or American agencies. But regular signed articles, sometimes from an outside contributor, do deal with major matters of national policy. Not long before the 1964 election, for instance, the *Sketch* published a scathing attack on the then Foreign Minister, Dr. Jaja Wachuku, for his policy over the Congo. And the paper regularly devotes a whole page to "Our Readers' Views."
> (66)

Having spent nine months in Nigeria in 1972-73, I feel I can speak with some authority on the Nigerian press. My claim to instant expertise rests on the half hour or so I devoted each day to reading Nigerian newspapers. I subscribed to five dailies from different parts of the country—the Lagos *Daily Times*, the Ibadan *Daily Sketch*, Kaduna's *New Nigerian*, Benin City's *Observer*, and Enugu's *Renaissance*—and when the newsboy couldn't bring one or more of these because of strikes, shortages, regional holidays or trouble with his bicycle, he would fill in with the *West African Pilot* from Lagos, the *Nigerian Tribune* from Ibadan, the *Nigerian Tide* from Port Harcourt, or any of a half-dozen other, less widely read dailies. On weekends he brought the *Sunday Post*, the *Sunday Times*, the *Sunday Observer*, the *Sunday Sketch*, the notorious *Lagos Weekend*, and sometimes a slick new pulp publication called *Sunday Punch* which invariably featured a half-naked girl on page one and headlines in orange ink. He was very considerate, this free-wheeling news pedaler. He knew I was hooked.

For the next few weeks I read almost every inch of every paper—news, editorials, feature articles, syndicated columns, letters to the editor, public announcements, commercial and classified ads, obituaries, memorials to the not-so-recently deceased, advice to the lovelorn, favorite recipes, cricket scores, captions, fillers, everything. Since some of these items didn't vary much from day to day or from daily to daily, I eventually developed the habit of reading one or two papers fairly carefully and skimming the rest. There were occasions when I hunted— sometimes in vain—for detailed accounts of news I had heard broadcast on the radio, especially stories having to do with the Munich Olympics, the presidential elections in the United States, and the opening chapters in the Watergate saga, but to satisfy this craving for admittedly exotic foreign fare, I finally had to break down and ask my three-speed supplier to bring copies of *Time* and *Newsweek* every week too. Nigerian newspapers were fine for Nigerian news, but they had a tendency to turn their backs on the rest of the world. After about three months I found I could pick up the average Nigerian newspaper and read everything that interested me in roughly thirty seconds. But I never stopped reading them and I never once considered stopping my subscriptions, for, if nothing else, Nigerian newspapers were extremely addictive. I doubt that anyone exposed to them regularly over a period of time could ever give them up entirely without losing some joy in life.

What makes them so compulsively habit-forming, I suspect, is their headlines. Even when the news is dull, the opinion columns trite, the letters to the editor insipid, the headlines sparkle. One never knows what curious conjunction of words is likely to leap off the next page in one-inch type. Reading a Nigerian newspaper cover to cover may become a tedious pastime after a month but skimming one never ceases to be a delight. The roving eye is being constantly ambushed by the unexpected, arrested by the graphically gregarious, or completely immobilized by the comically incongruous. After a particularly pungent headline, the news story following is bound to seem an anti-climax. Indeed, the only way to really enjoy Nigerian newspapers, the only way to develop a taste for them so as to savor all their outrageous delights like a jaded connoisseur, is to avoid reading the smaller print. Look not beyond the largest letters on the page.

Once I learned this simple lesson, reading newspapers in Nigeria became high adventure. Every day was a treasure hunt for the roughest gems. These I shared not only with my wife, children, and associates in Ibadan but also with my sister and brother-in-law in Texas. Each Monday I would airmail them an envelope stuffed with the previous week's quota of typographical trophies. Postage on these packets would usually run about sixty kobo (nearly a dollar), but in the most productive weeks it sometimes amounted to as much as one naira, fifty kobo (approximately $2.30). Nevertheless, I think the investment was well worth the expense, for it not only brought a lot of happiness to the folks back home but also established in Austin, Texas, a permanent archive of carefully selected Nigerian newspaper headlines on which social scientists, cultural anthropologists, folklorists, historians, psychologists, media specialists, professors of the fine arts, philosophers, ethno-aestheticians and other curious scholars could test their latest theories. I am, of course, aware that any collection of documents—particularly a selective collection—is apt to reveal as much about the collector as the material collected, but I am willing to run the risk of public self-exposure in the interest of advancing the frontiers of human knowledge. A larger collection gathered indiscriminately would have only befuddled the prospective researcher by glutting him with trivia. A Dean once asked me how many more such headlines could be garnered with unlimited resources of time and money. "There would be no problem raising a million," I told him, "but it would be wrong."

I would now like to open my files to all investigators so that suspicions and rumors about my activities in Nigeria can be laid to rest. I think the evidence I am about to present—evidence scrupulously selected and meticulously edited—will speak for itself, but to make sure everything is perfectly clear, I would like to say a few words in my own behalf. First, I want you to know that I accept full responsibility—but not blame—for what follows. Second, I assure you there has been absolutely no cover-up, no inflation of the facts, no recession in my efforts to determine the truth. Third, I have never used these documents as deductions or write-offs on my income tax, even though several authorities in the field have advised me they would make me worth less. Finally, although some of the actual documents may look like they have been through a paper shredder, they have not been altered or mutilated since being snipped from Nigerian newspapers. Having stated this, I wish to emphasize that I do not intend to resign myself to criticism which should be directed at other individuals and parties. I am resolved to fight for what I want believed, to search for the unimpeachable answer, even if this requires the ultimate sacrifice of allowing myself to become a Nigerian newspaper headline.

I suppose the best place to begin a survey of these materials would be with the "human interest" headlines, since these often appear on page one in the largest possible type. Any kind of extraordinary behavior is likely to be loudly trumpeted. For instance:

DEAD MAN RISES!
TWO-HEADED CHILD BORN IN P'HARCOURT
MAN DISPLAYS HUMAN FLESH FOR SALE
TAX COLLECTOR HACKED TO DEATH
MOTHER OF BABY WITH 3 FATHERS DIES
ABAKALIKI SOIL MEN DOWN BUCKETS
BULLYING HUSSY GETS A BITE IN HIS SECRET PLACE

At times the headlines can be rather grisly:

FISHERMAN MATCHETS 45-YEAR-OLD MUM TO DEATH IN
    ORON
TREE CRUSHES COUPLE IN BED TO DEATH
WOMAN SMASHED DEAD BY MINI BUS
FARMER ROASTED BY FARM FIRE
FOUR TO DIE FOR KILLING AND EATING 19-YEAR GIRL
HUMAN SKULL FOUND IN TOP COP'S HOUSE

There also appears to be a great deal of interest in serious breaches of social etiquette. Hardly a day goes by without some aberration of civilized human conduct being recorded for posterity:

GUEST STEALS ONLY CHILD OF HER HOST
ACCUSED MISTAKES ANOTHER'S WIFE FOR HIS GIRL
2 CALL-GIRLS STOP TRAFFIC AS THEY FIGHT OVER
    CUSTOMER
QUARREL OVER KOLANUT LANDS TWO WOMEN INTO A
    WELL
CHIEF IN PIG TUSSLE

Sometimes these quarrels are all in the family:

MAN BITES WIFE 'IN SELF-DEFENCE'
BROTHER ACCUSED OF SELLING SISTER
HUSBAND LOSES BID TO EJECT WIFE
FATHER TAKES SON TO COURT FOR STEALING

Of course, some of these headlines could be found in any regional or international newspaper. They are not all uniquely Nigerian. But the sheer quantity of such leaders in the Nigerian press leads one to suspect that it would be difficult to stumble upon so many in such concentration anywhere else in the world. There are also an incredible number of comic headlines, some of which may not have been intended as humorous:

COURT RISES AS WITNESS COLLAPSES
NEW BODY LAUNCHED FOR OLD GUIDES
TROUSERS WERE A BURGLAR'S DOWNFALL
STUDENT'S UNREST—A DISTURBING PHENOMENON
FIRE EXTINGUISHER—A MUST FOR EVERY BEER PARLOUR
CHIEF WHO ADMITS KILLING 200 FEARS REVENGE

There are also some very original and creative uses of English clichés, many of them quite deliberate distortions of the standard form:

HERE IS MUD IN YOUR FACE
LET SLEEPING DONS LIE
THE TASTE OF THE PUDDING IS IN THE EATING

Certain of these verbal formulae appear to bear the imprint of African oral tradition:

MAY YOUR SHADOW NEVER GROW LESS
MORE GREASE TO YOUR ELBOW
GROW OLD GRACEFULLY LIKE THE SCORPION
NO PLANK NO HOUSE

Others are straightforward aphorisms with an obvious moral:

DEATH IS NOT THE END OF THE WORLD
STEALING IS A BAD HABIT
IT'S STUPID TO COMMIT SUICIDE
A DOSE OF PUB-CRAWLING IS GOOD FOR YOU

Another category of headlines might be called warnings or expostulations. These sometimes have a stern, menacing tone:

IF SINNERS ENTICE YOU, CONSENT NOT
DON'T ASSAULT REVENUE COLLECTORS
DON'T BRIBE REFUSE MEN
DON'T PANIC WHEN KID HAS HERNIA
WATCH IT! YOU MAY HAVE A DUD
PUNTERS, BEWARE OF FAKE NAPS!

Allied to these exhortations are the headlines which voice complaints or discontents. These are usually quite direct:

OUR RAILWAY SYSTEM IS ONLY FIT FOR THE MUSEUM
DOCTORS ARE BECOMING SWOLLEN HEADED
PROPHETS SHOULD PAY TAX

Many such headlines glare out from the "letters to the editor" column which is probably the most moralistic and verbally vehement section of any Nigerian newspaper. The milder letters are given cool captions such as:

I DISAGREE WITH SOME POINTS RAISED
THAT ANNOUNCEMENT IS VERY DISTURBING
THAT ATTACK ON TEACHERS IS RATHER UNFORTUNATE
LET'S HOPE THAT THE RUBBISH WILL NOT RETURN TO ITS
    FORMER ABODE
RECTIFY THE ANOMALY

But the angrier letters are preceded by blunt, insistent statements or demands:

LET'S STOP THESE DIRTY DEALS NOW
SAVE US FROM THE LANDLORDS
KEEP THE COWS OFF
WE ARE NOT IMPRESSED!
THAT DEFENCE LEAKS VERY BADLY

The emphasis on public and private morality so pronounced in these letters is further reinforced by reports of speeches given by important officials and dignitaries. The headlines often make it appear that the speakers have a rather low opinion of the personal habits and professional practices of some of the groups they address, for they keep reminding members of these groups to behave as anyone would normally expect them to behave. For instance:

JUDGES URGED TO BE FAIR
OFFICIALS URGED TO BE HONEST
MUSLIMS TOLD TO BE CLEAN
NIGERIAN STUDENTS URGED TO THINK
BUSINESSMEN URGED TO ESCHEW GREEDINESS
BANKS TOLD TO ENHANCE THE ECONOMY
NATIONAL CENSUS BOARD TOLD TO BE BROAD-MINDED
AUDITORS WARNED NOT TO NEGLECT THEIR SACRED
DUTY

The heavy-handed didacticism of these speakers is surpassed only by the preaching of priests, ministers, prophets and Christian laymen who write religious columns or letters to the editor in the Nigerian press. One usually finds conventional theological messages prefacing many of these offerings, but occasionally the headlines are deliberately provocative, even to the point of sounding sacrilegious.

REINCARNATION IS FACTUAL
OF COURSE, THE POPE IS INFALLIBLE
THE BIBLE WAS NOT WRITTEN BY GOD
THE GARDEN OF EDEN WAS IN NIGERIA
THE WORLD IS BUILT BY HERETICS

Of course, many of these shocking headlines are intended simply to capture the reader's attention or to simulate curiosity. The story beneath a bizarre banner may turn out to be a disappointingly conventional account of the same old stuff one has read before. A favorite tactic is to phrase the headline as a question:

> IS THE AFRICAN A BLACK MAN?
> WILL MORE BREWERIES SOLVE THE BEER PROBLEM?
> ARE WOMEN REALLY THE WEAKER SEX?
> ARE NIGERIAN GIRLS TOO EXPENSIVE?
> HOW RELIABLE IS YOUR FUEL PUMP?
> IS THERE JUJU IN FOOTBALL?
> HOW DO TORTOISES MATE?
> AND WHO IS SMILING FROM THE GRAVE?

At times the questions are furnished with firm answers:

> ARE YOU YOUNG, INTELLIGENT, PRETTY AND RICH?—THEN
>   YOU'VE HAD IT
> THE COMMON MAN? HE'S EVER SO COMMON HERE
> PLATONIC FRIENDSHIP? NO SUCH THING IN OUR SOCIETY

Another attention-getting ploy is to quote unusual statements made by people in the news:

> "HE TOLD ME HIS BROTHER PRINTS MONEY"
> "BEER IS NOT DEATH TO ME"
> MAN ACCUSED OF STEALING SAYS: "I'M QUITE NORMAL"
> "THE SCHOOL TOILET WAS MY CHURCH"

Some of the most colorful questions and quotations in headlines come from the sections of the paper devoted to the personal problems of readers. Most Nigerian newspapers have the equivalent of a "Dear Abby" column in which an experienced and sophisticated woman of the world offers advice to the lovelorn.[2] Several papers also have medical columns where letters from readers with worrisome physical symptoms are answered by an anonymous doctor, supposedly a well-qualified physician. The *Sunday Observer* used to combine both columns in a page called "HELP!" which had the reassuring subtitle: "All your problems are solved on this page." The headlines here were often quite revealing:

AM I NORMAL?
CAN I HAVE KIDDIES WITH ONE TESTIS?
SHOULD I COMMIT SUICIDE OR PACK AWAY FROM HIS
   HOUSE?
MY MIND IS POISONED
MY MOUTH IS BECOMING WIDER
PEOPLE LEAN AWAY WHEN I TALK
HELP! I HAVE LICE IN MY PUBIC HAIR
NO GIRL FRIEND, MY THING BENT
HE TRIED TO LOVE ME WITHOUT GIFTS
I DON'T KNOW WHICH OF MY WIVES IS A WITCH

Since some of the readers who write in for advice are preoccupied with what they regard as socially devastating biological, sexual and amatory failures, it is not surprising that Nigerian newspapers frequently carry articles devoted to sex education of one sort or another. These tend to range all the way from professional tips on physiological behavior (e.g., HINTS ON A GOOD FOREPLAY; SWINGERS GUIDE—HOW TO BE A GOOD BED PARTNER; THE UNMARRIED NEEDS FAMILY PLANNING TOO; SOME TRANQUILIZERS AFFECT THE GENITAL ORGANS) to suggestions on courtship strategies (e.g., HOW TO WIN THE LOVE GAME WITHOUT REALLY TRYING; THE DIALECTICS OF FLIRTATION; CASSETTE MUSIC IS AN AID TO WOOING A GIRL; CUDDLE HIM AFTER A BLACK EYE) to pep-talks for unmarried women (e.g., WE AFRICAN WOMEN ARE SIMPLY SUPER; BE COURAGEOUS SPINSTERS—GOOD DAYS ARE STILL AHEAD; YOU DON'T HAVE TO BE VULGAR TO ATTRACT MEN; FLIRTATION IS A TENSION-RELIEVING EXERCISE) to philosophical remarks on the immorality of modern times (MARRIAGES ARE NO LONGER MADE IN HEAVEN; ADULTERY IS HERE TO STAY; SEX—HOW IT CAN RUIN YOUR LIFE; THE DRIFT TO MORAL

DISASTER). The emphasis in most of these "educational" articles is on how to survive and perhaps even thrive in the overcharged atmosphere of Nigerian cities after dark.

There are also numerous news stories on peculiar liaisons:

MADAM TUCKS IN HER HOUSEBOY!
SEX-THIRSTY WIFE TAKES PUPPY TO BED
DRIVER ON TRIAL OVER BID TO RAPE BOSS'S DAUGHTER
    AGED FOUR
MAN RAPES WIFE'S MOTHER
AMPUTEE TO SERVE 2 YEARS FOR RAPE

Quite a few headlines play upon the reader's interest in anything unusual having to do with sex or romantic relationships:

YOUNG WIFE LOCKS UP HER MAN'S THING
OLD PAPPY, 92, IS KILLED BY JEALOUS LOVER
THE BITTER THING ABOUT GO-GO GIRLS
WHITE GIRLS CAN GO ANYWHERE IN PYJAMAS
HARLOTS KICK AGAINST CUT IN "SHORT TIME" INCOME
LEBANESE LOVE OUR GOATS AND WOMEN
SEAWEED KEEPS WOMEN CHEEKY

Allied to this obsession with sex in the Nigerian press is a morbid fascination with crime and punishment. Nigerian newspapers, like B-grade news media throughout the world, make a practice of stationing reporters at courts so the latest high crimes and misdemeanors can be retailed in detail in the next morning's edition. Sometimes only the most eccentric cases make the headlines:

COUPLE ARRESTED FOR HAVING SEX OPENLY AT BEACH
JOE HIDES WATCHES IN ANUS, TRIBUNAL TOLD
HOUSEWIFE WHO POURED HOT WATER ON PREGNANT
    WOMAN CONVICTED
FATHER WHO TIED CHILD TO BUCKET FINED ₦5
"DIRTYMAN" JAILED 5 YEARS

To balance all this bad and scandalous news, there are, of course, some headlines which put the accent on the positive. A random sampling of these might include:

A NEW JESUS!
IBADAN GETS THIRD COMFORT STATION
DAHOMEY COUP IS SOOTHING
LUNATICS GET HAIRCUT
PRIESTS UPLIFTED
OUR SALARY IS FAT
WE ARE THE GREATEST

The drawings and photographs which accompany such proclamations are often too funny for words. Sometimes an incongruous caption will appear beneath a picture of a famous personality; for example, a shot of Commander Diete-Spiff, Governor of the Rivers State, once ended up over a boldface headline that read "SUBSIDIZED FERTILIZER," and a flattering photo of broadly smiling Brigadier K.J. Esuene, Governor of the South-Eastern State, got placed above the legend: "He is sad over the tragic incident." But my favorites always appeared on the political pages. During the American presidential election, it was not at all uncommon to see hilariously antiquated photographs of Richard Nixon or to discover that the captions beneath separate pictures of Nixon and McGovern waving to crowds of enthusiastic supporters had been transposed. In one paper the headline "KENNEDY JOINS MCGOVERN CAMPAIGN" was illustrated with a shot of the late Robert Kennedy, and in another a photograph of grim-faced Alexei Kosygin appeared over the inscription "President Nixon (U.S.A.)." It was this kind of happy surprise every morning that got my days in Nigeria off to a good start. Nigerian newspapers did more to perk me up than any cup of coffee could.

Nigerians appear to thoroughly enjoy their newspapers, too. At least they continue buying them, which is one indication that they are interested in reading them and willing to forgive their characteristic peccadilloes. Occasionally Nigerians will complain about the inadequacies of their newspapers but they tend to do this in the very newspapers concerned, an encouraging sign that someone up there in the editor's office is listening. Many of the faults they cite will no doubt be remedied n the next decade or two as reporters, typesetters and proofreaders for Nigerian newspapers become better educated, better trained and better equipped with modern machinery. However, whether Nigerian newspapers will ever lose their flair for the sensational or their zest for memorable phrases is an open question, for they seem to pride themselves on achieving a truly Nigerian personality by speaking out uninhibitedly in a popular idiom. The way they describe themselves in their own advertisements is evidence of this:

THE *SUNDAY SKETCH* IS A TREMENDOUSLY EXCITING NEWSPAPER. EVERY THING IT HAUDLES [sic], IT DOES DRAMATICALLY. VASTLY ENTERTAINING, EDUCATIVE AND QUITE IRRESISTIBLE.

The Lagos *Daily Times*, probably the most influential paper in the country in the 1970s, billed itself as

THE KIND OF NEWSPAPER YOU HAVE BEEN DREAMING OF READING. PUNGENT, FEARLESS, WELL-REASONED EDITORIALS FEATURES BY EXPERTS. UP-TO-DATE FACTUAL NEWS, CAPTIVATING PICTURES AND A LOT MORE IT IS WHAT A POPULAR NEWSPAPER SHOULD BE [sic]

If this is the kind of newspaper Nigerians want, this is the kind they are likely to get for some time to come. The exuberant, quirky, comical headlines will not stop because they are what makes a popular newspaper pop.

In a column in one of the papers I read daily someone once said, "My recommendation for anyone who is trying to understand the Nigerian is to read Nigerian newspapers more closely." After nine months in Nigeria, I disagree. My own recommendation would be to hold Nigerian newspapers at arms' length and read only the headlines. They never tell the whole story but—like campus streakers—they can provide glimpses of what might otherwise be hidden, hard to uncover, and difficult to lay one's hands on.

---

[1] For the benefit of those unfamiliar with this American pastime, it is perhaps sufficient to state that *Time* once defined "streaking" as "the art of the point-to-point dash in the buff." (18 March 1974: 58)

[2] For Zambian examples of this genre, see Hall.

Documents

agunwa's Opinions on Fiction

The late Chief Daniel Olorunfemi Fagunwa is undoubtedly the most important author in Yoruba literature. According to informed critics who have read his works in the language in which they were written, he has no equal as a raconteur and has never been surpassed as a stylist. Ayo Bamgbose, in the first book published on his fiction, states that "Apart from his skill as a story-teller, Fagunwa's main claim to greatness as a Yoruba novelist is his language" (1974: 108). Ulli Beier, Abiola Irele, A. Olubummo and Afolabi Olabimtan have voiced essentially the same opinion. All consider Fagunwa to be remarkably gifted in powers of invention and expression.

It is always interesting to read what a renowned author has said or written about the art of writing because the statements he makes tend to reveal something about the attitudes and principles that underlie his own work. How did a storyteller like Fagunwa view fiction? What kind of story did he most enjoy reading? What did he see as the purpose of literature? What role did he feel the writer should play in society? What, in short, was his literary philosophy?

Fortunately, we can attempt to answer these questions today because Fagunwa tried to answer them more than thirty years ago in a brief article published in a Ministry of Education journal called *Teachers' Monthly*. Here is the complete text of that article:

Writing a Novel
by
D.O. Fagunwa

Teachers often ask questions on the writing of a novel. Of late, these questions have increased. How do novelists produce their works? What is the difference between a publisher and a printer? What are phantasia novels? etc. Here an attempt is made to reply some of these questions, and the reply represents my own personal opinion.

A novel is a written prose fiction. It has developed from the word "romance" which is applicable to verse as well. Also we sometimes hear of "Novels in Verse." In other words the writing of a long story in a connected form, which, though it had not happened, is presented as though it, in fact, had happened, may be regarded as a novel.

The aim of a novelist is to present to the public something interesting to read, and the success or failure of a novel lies in how far it can get hold of its readers and compel them to read on. This is why its place is of special importance in a community such as ours where people as a rule do not read works in their own languages except in so far as they have a bearing on the passing of this or that examination.

Now, all aspects of life do not interest people equally. Love for instance interests most people. We like to love and be loved. We also like to watch those who are loving or being loved. Money interests all: we need at least some for our existence and so we are interested further in the rich and the poor. Adventure interests some but not all. We hear of people who walk long distances, swim wide expanse of water or climb mountains. The mysterious interests us in one way or another. What for instance happens to us after death? Is it true that if we behave well on earth, we go to Paradise and otherwise to hell? Are there ghosts? Do spirits inhabit trees, rocks, rivers, streams etc.? What a novelist does is to present one or more of these aspects of life and weave a long story around whichever he takes.

All these aspects of life are not equally difficult to write about. A novel based on love is not very difficult to write because even if all the true stories of love we hear are written and joined, they easily look like fiction. Equally a novel based on money is not very difficult to write since stories connected with misappropriation of money are common in real life.

A novel which involves the mysterious is perhaps the most difficult to write. In such a case the writer goes really into the world of imagination and therefore it is necessary for him to have had an inborn gift of imagination. In literary history, only few brains had produced this type of writing and the products have lived long.

John Bunyan has been described as the father of English novels. His *Pilgrim's Progress* describes no other thing than the journey from this world to the world to come. So is Spenser's *Faerie Queene* a novel in verse.

The term "Phantasia novels" is an invention used for describing novels written in African languages in Nigeria but, in literary language, I have never heard of that term. However, I know the type of novels that the majority of Western Nigerians have written, my having been a long time in the Publications Section of this Ministry, and being responsible for reading and assessing Government publications has placed me in a position to know what our people write about.

Let me say, in the first place that it is not correct to say that all Nigerian novels have something of phantasy in them but the majority do. I usually term these Spenserian because they so much resemble the works of an English writer, whose works were published in the late sixteenth and early seventeenth century A.D., called Edmund Spenser. The fact about them is that if well handled they have a peculiarly forceful way of driving an idea home. They interest Nigerian readers a good deal and I have always encouraged rather than discouraged them. Compare this personification in Book I of Spenser's *Faerie Queene*. In Spenser's view, the reformed Church was full of misdeeds. He does not as a result describe these acts of omission and commission in mere words, but instead, he personifies Error as a horrible monster half-serpent half-woman living in a dark, filthy cave, to be fought by a knight who himself was the son of a fairy. Here, when everything of the misdeeds of the Church could have been forgotten, the picture of this monster would remain in the mind.

As has been pointed out above, our duty is to present to our readers what we know will interest them. We should not merely copy others but should give first consideration to the need of our society. Experience has shown that British humour is not the same as the African's, and while it is doubtful whether the British would like an element of phantasy in a novel, surely some of the continentals will do. Besides, there is nothing wrong in making our own kind of writing our special contribution to the literary history of the world. Nigerian society is broadly divided into two, namely, the educated section and the non-educated, (those who had been to school and those who have never been). A big slice of the former together with nearly all the latter believe in juju, spirits, ghosts etc., and a novelist should take an account of this. (12)

It is worth noting that Fagunwa puts his emphasis on invention, not on style. In fact, hardly a word is said about the manner in which an author ought to express himself. Fagunwa evidently placed matter before manner, subject before style, in his literary scale of values. He knew that every novelist aspires "to present to the public something interesting to read," but he felt that the best way for any writer to attempt to fulfill this aspiration was through careful selection of a theme that would have widespread popular appeal. Money and love were not only intrinsically interesting subjects but were also quite easy to write about because everyone knew something about them from firsthand experience. Adventure stories, on the other hand, did not have universal appeal but were of interest to some readers. The kind of fiction that fascinated people "in one way or another" but was "perhaps the most difficult to write" because it required "an inborn gift of imagination" was the kind that Fagunwa himself most favored and always wrote—a kind known then in Western Nigeria as the "Phantasia novel."

As its name implied, the Phantasia novel contained elements of fantasy derived from the "world of imagination." It was not rooted in tangible mundane realities but was concerned with "the mysterious"—that is, with otherworldly notions that could not be verified empirically. Notice that Fagunwa defines "the mysterious" as a realm of metaphysical speculation. He is not interested in writing whodunits, gothic romances, or science fiction. His eye is fixed on the larger mysteries of life and death, flesh and spirit, essence and existence. "What for instance happens to us after death? Is it true that if we behave well on earth we go to Paradise and otherwise to hell? Are there ghosts? Do spirits inhabit trees, rocks, rivers, streams etc.?" Fagunwa, Nigeria's foremost Phantasia novelist, was a transcendentalist at heart.

This becomes even clearer when he cites examples of English fiction concerned with "the mysterious." The first work mentioned, John Bunyan's *The Pilgrim's Progress*, is not at all surprising because Bunyan has frequently been discussed as an important source of inspiration for Fagunwa (Bamgbose 24-26; Lindfors 1970: 57-65). But Spenser's *The Faerie Queene*, an allegorical verse epic antedating *The Pilgrim's Progress* by nearly a century, comes as a mild shock because one does not expect that someone with Fagunwa's limited educational background (primary school plus three years at a teachers' training college) would have been exposed to this venerable classic. Certainly no literary critic or commentator on Fagunwa's writing has ever mentioned it as being among the books that had an impact on him. Bamgbose, who devotes an entire chapter of his book to Fagunwa's "Background and Sources" (1974: 8-30), cites *The Odyssey*, classical Greek mythology, the *Arabian Nights*, Aesop's *Fables*, Marlowe's *Doctor Faustus*, Defoe's *Robinson Crusoe*, and scenes from Shakespeare, Milton and Chaucer as sources of inspiration for Fagunwa, but he makes no mention of Spenser. Yet in retrospect, Fagunwa's tribute to Spenser seems perfectly natural and right. *The Faerie Queene* displays precisely the kind of vivid didactic transcendentalism that makes both Bunyan's *The Pilgrim's Progress* and Fagunwa's *The Forest of a Thousand Daemons* so memorable. All three are episodic religious parables that imaginatively explore "the mysterious" through allegory. All three attempt to instruct as well as entertain.

Fagunwa evidently felt that literature, even at its most diverting and pleasurable, ought to have a serious purpose. In fact, he considered it the writer's duty to capture the attention of readers and "compel them to read on" for their own edification and enjoyment. If literature did nothing more than to promote greater literacy among people who were unaccustomed to reading outside of school, it would justify its existence. But a larger purpose would be served if the author could induce the educated and non-educated to ponder some of the big questions of life. This, Fagunwa felt, could be accomplished through adroit use of "phantasy." The underlying motive was not to help readers escape from the realities of life but to lead them to confront the larger spiritual realities in which their lives were ultimately rooted. By making readers think as well as feel, the writer would improve the quality of their intellectual and imaginative experience.

But one couldn't accomplish all this through dull writing. The writer certainly shouldn't bore his audience. This is where his own "inborn gift of imagination" was of such crucial importance. The writer couldn't fulfill his responsibilities to his fellow man if he wrote uninteresting stories or if he borrowed his material from abroad. "We should not merely copy others but should give first consideration to the need of our society." The author, in other words, should write original fiction custom-tailored to suit the aesthetic preferences of Nigerian readers. His matter and his manner should be uncompromisingly African. Only if he achieved this self-confidence and rare creative independence could he make a profound impact on his society. And only then would he stand a chance of earning immortality by "making our own kind of writing our special contribution to the world."

Fagunwa's literary philosophy reveals him to be an artist somewhat ahead of his times. In modern parlance we might call him a "committed writer," a "cultural nationalist," or a purveyor of "black consciousness" in literature. At a time when many other African authors were addressing their messages to Europe and experimenting with foreign literary forms and fashions, Fagunwa was intent on speaking to his own people in an imaginative idiom they could understand and appreciate. He affirmed the value of African verbal traditions even while exploring the relevance and utility of imported modes of expressive art. He combined indigenous morality with Christianity, the folktale with allegory and parable, politics and metaphysics with art, creating in the process his own distinctive genre of didactic, transcendental prose fiction. He was Nigeria's first classic storyteller and first modern novelist, and it unlikely that his narratives will ever be forgotten.

Ogunde on Ogunde: Two Autobiographical Statements

Hubert Ogunde (1916-1990), considered the "father" of Yoruba operatic theater (Adedeji 135), is one of Africa's better known entertainers and showmen. In Nigeria he was long regarded as a living legend who almost single-handedly pioneered the professional development of a popular art form called the Concert Party, a thoroughly African mode of musical comedy (Owomoyela 1971; cf. Ricard). One informed commentator has stated quite matter-of-factly that "Professional theatre in Yoruba begins with Hubert Ogunde" (Beier 1967: 245). As a performer, producer, and promoter of indigenous stage entertainment, he remained active for more than forty years, becoming in the process a kind of national institution. It was only fitting that at the end of his career he was elected President of the Union of Nigerian Dramatists and Playwrights and made Director of the National Troupe at the National Theatre in Lagos. When he died a few years later, the Nigerian press was filled with tributes honoring him for his contributions to the cultural life of the nation (see, e.g., Soyinka 1990).

There has been one substantial book on Ogunde (Clark) and another on the Yoruba traveling theater (Jeyifo) plus a number of essays published on him in biographical dictionaries (Jahn, et al 290-292; Herdeck 316-318), professional journals (e.g., Anpe), and popular magazines (e.g., Anon. 1964, 1965, 1970, 1972). Yet despite everything that has been written about him and his contribution to African drama, there are hardly any primary sources to which one can turn for basic biographical information on the man and his career. Most scholars tend to repeat the remarks of observers based in Nigeria who either knew Ogunde personally or interviewed him about his life and activities (e.g., Graham-White 149-150). So far as I have been able to determine only a single interview with him has been published in western academic media, and that one appeared in a French translation! (Bertrand). It may therefore be of some value to reproduce two autobiographical statements by Ogunde that appeared some years ago in Nigerian popular magazines. The first was issued in two installments in the *TV Times and Radio News*, a weekly publication of the Lagos *Daily Times* (Ogunde 1960). The second appeared thirteen years later in *New Era*, a magazine published in what was then the East Central State of Nigeria (Ogunde 1973).

There are several discrepancies in these two accounts (noted in brackets in the second) which may be due to printing or reporting errors. A comparison with other sources of biographical information suggests that the longer statement in the *TV Times and Radio News* is the more trustworthy. Nevertheless, both accounts are valuable for the revealing light they shed on Ogunde's career and personality.

The Life of Hubert Ogunde
Part One

I have had a very successful career in show business. Although it has been satisfying, my life as a showman has not been very exciting but it hasn't been a dull life either.

I am happy I took to the stage at the time I did. For today, although there aren't many Nigerians in the profession yet, I am beginning to see what great prospects lie ahead for the showman in this country.

Nigerians are great lovers of fun and anyone who has a talent for entertaining others has a bright future in this country.

I was born at Ososa, a little village four miles west of Ijebu Ode in Western Nigeria, in 1916. My mother was a pagan at the time I was born. She was later converted to Christianity.

My father, Jeremiah D. Ogunde, was a pastor at the Baptist Church at Ijebu-Ife, about sixty miles from my home. It is strange how he came to marry a pagan.

My mother's pagan connections had tremendous influence on my early life. Her father was an Ife [Ifa?] priest.

In those days singing, drumming and dancing were regular features of Ife festivals. As I had to stay most of the times with my mother, she took me along with her each time she was attending a pagan festival.

My grandfather—the Ife priest—also had a special liking for me and wanted me at his side always. I too loved the old man and loved to be at his side when he was performing his Ife ceremonies.

It was by being constantly at the old man's side watching him pouring out his incantations and listening to the songs and drums of the pagans that I first developed interest in juju music and plays.

I started schooling in 1926 at the Baptist School Ife where my father, in addition to being the pastor in charge of the mission, was also the headmaster of the school. He was also the school's organist.

Soon I joined the school's choir. This was my second inspiration in my journey to music.

The church songs of those days were soul-rendering. For me it had its special charm.

Here I was, a youth versed, as I could claim to be then, in juju music and used to the altar of the Ife priest. I had eaten fowls and sheep slaughtered in pagan festivals and enjoyed them to the full. Then I was in church, singing songs of praise to God and denouncing the juju man and his ways.

The effect on me was too much for words. Thanks to God that I was not biased either way.

As small as I was then, I began to see that I could blend the charms and splendour of the church house and the colourful solemnity of the Ife altar and use it to good advantage.

It was such a rich experience and one I shall ever be grateful that I had.

1933 was my last year in school—as a pupil. That was the African Bethel School, Ijebu Ode.

The following year, 1934, I was employed as a teacher in the St. John's C.M.S. School, in my hometown, Ososa, on a commencing salary of TEN SHILLINGS a month.

It was as a teacher that I started to give serious attention to music. My tutors were my school's organist, Mr. G.A. Adenuga, and my father.

I taught for eight years and was also an organist for eight years.

Then it was a special advantage for a teacher to know how to play the organ. For the schools then were owned by the church and the pastors and clergymen who ran the affairs of the school took it as an integral part of the church.

So it was not enough to know your subjects as a teacher. You had to know nearly everything about the church in order to progress.

And because the Church then was built on songs, the organist was looked upon as the live wire of the place. Such was the position I enjoyed for eight years in Abeokuta and Ijebu Provinces where I was most of the time.

It was at the Oke Ona United School Abeokuta that I first organised a band. The band had forty-two members.

We used bugles and flutes. The flutes we used were like the ones used by the Army and the Police.

Soon the band became very popular all over the province. My personal popularity grew with that of the band. I was liked and talked about by nearly everybody. But it was not without its consequences.

The girls came in. They clung around me. And what names did they not call me! "Darling"; "honey"; "sweetie"; "mine".

From every corner of Abeokuta reports flowed in of girls fighting and quarrelling because of Hubert Ogunde. Often the quarrels ended up in the Police station.

I became a regular visitor to the Abeokuta Police Station—just to say what I knew about the girls who had fought over me. And often they were girls whose faces I could not remember having seen before.

In the midst of fellow boys I appeared pleased to be the talk of the town.

But in my sober moments and at home I felt very embarrassed about it all. The position remained so for three years.

When the school closed for the Christmas holiday in 1941 I went to Ibadan to visit a brother. This visit made its own mark in my life. For it was during that time that I applied and became a policeman!

This was how it happened:

It was a dull afternoon. I was strolling past the Dugbe Market when I saw a huge crowd in the Police Barracks, which was close by. I grew curious.

"What is it?", I asked a man who was passing by at the time.

"Oh," he said casually, "They are recruiting young men for the Force".

"Recruiting young men for the Police Force?" , I asked myself.

I had never thought of joining the force before then although I had always admired the smart uniforms of policemen especially when they were on parade.

I stood still for a while watching what was going on in the barracks. There wasn't much activity in the place. There were young men, some of them looking very hungry and underfed.

Others lined up in a queue. Then I decided to try my luck. What it was that pushed me to that decision, I cannot say.

I jumped into the market, bought a sheet of foolscap paper, bent over my knees and drafted an application. Then I hurried to the barracks to join the Nigerian Police Force. There were over 500 in the queue.

Soon an officer, whose muscles looked as tough as those of a bullfighter, appeared on the scene.

We moved nearer and the officer began what I considered was a most careful examination of our physical standing. Finally he selected forty of us.

We were conducted to a room where a written test was set for us. I scored the highest marks in the test and was finally chosen along with three others to join the Police Force.

We were sent to the then Police Training College in Enugu. That was in 1942.

Of course, I did not write back to my school to resign my appointment!

After my training I was posted to Ibadan. I worked as a traffic officer, then I was moved to the Criminal Investigations Department and in 1943 I was transferred to Lagos.

Coming to Lagos in 1943 brought a spectacular change to my life.

The Life of Hubert Ogunde
Part Two

While in the Police Force I was a member of the Aladoro Church, Lagos. I took such active interest in the activities of the Church that later in 1943 I was commissioned to write a Service of Songs for the Church.

A Service of Songs is just a list of songs for use on various occasions. This was thought a particularly important assignment because the Aladoro Church attached so much importance to songs.

I took up the job enthusiastically for I knew that a successful discharge of it would make me a hero in the church. What I did not realise then was that the writing of the Service of Songs would open a new world to me.

Something struck me when I started assembling songs for the book. I thought it was not enough to sing songs. There must be action to make it lively. There were several passages in the songs I had gathered and in the Bible which I was also studying intensely which could be dramatised successfully.

For some days I held up the preparation of the book, thinking how to add "life" to the Songs. Soon I found myself writing my first play "The Garden of Eden." It was staged in the Glover Memorial Hall, Lagos, on June 12, 1944, by members of the Aladoro Church.

The success of this play inspired me to write my second play "Africa and God". Later in the same year (1944) I wrote and directed the staging of "Israel in Egypt" and "Nebukanezzer's Reign."

1945 was another year of writing of plays for me. I wrote "Strike and Hunger"; "Human Parasites"; "Journey to Heaven"; "The Black Forest"; and "King Solomon." All the plays were based on themes in the Bible and in other religious works.

I was invalided from the Police Force in 1945 after I had attained the rank of Second Class Constable. It is not true, as has been said in many quarters, that I reached the inspectorate grade in the Force.

Perhaps what the friends who placed me so high meant to say was that the second class constable of those days is the equivalent of the sub inspector of today.

Following my invaliding from the Police Force I turned a professional showman. But most of my plays continued to depict religious thoughts.

I broke into a new field in 1946 when I wrote and dramatised "Herbert Macaulay" in memory of the greatest of Nigerian patriots Herbert Samuel Heelas Macaulay who died earlier in the year. I followed that up with "Mr. Devil's Money" and "The Tiger's Empire".

I was, by standards obtaining in the country, doing fine as a playwright. But I knew that I had a long way to go before I could be a truly professional playwright and showman. Daily I wanted to go to Europe and study drama. I was convinced that an overseas study course would greatly add to the show talents which I already possessed.

I beat my own procrastination in 1947 and went to England and was lucky to be admitted in the Buddy Bradley School of Dancing at the Piccadilly Circus, London. During my stay there I had the opportunity of visiting several theatres and film studios in the United Kingdom and later I went to Paris on a sight-seeing trip.

Returning to Nigeria towards the end of the year I wrote more plays—"Towards Liberty" and "Yours Forever". The name Hubert Ogunde was now becoming fairly well known in the country. To establish myself firmly I used the whole of 1948 for tours to advertise myself and my plays. I visited Ghana and the Ivory Coast. The big receptions I received encouraged me greatly. The crowd at Ivory Coast was so big that I had to make the gate fee ONE POUND flat. Yet the hall was packed to capacity.

Perhaps I have been giving you too much of the rosy side of my life. Let's go back now in 1946 for a little excitement.

I was in Jos, Northern Nigeria. I had gone there during my Northern tour to stage the play "Strike and Hunger". The play concerned the 1945 general strike by Nigerian workers. The strike brought misery to many homes and nearly brought many Government and commercial businesses to a halt.

Suddenly in the middle of the play policemen swooped on me and my party and we were dragged to the local police station where we were arrested and locked up in cells. Nothing so stunned me as that arrest. I just did not understand it at all. I thought it was a dream.

I was charged with attempting to incite His Majesty's subjects to disorder. The court found me guilty and I was fined a total of £125!

Before the Jos incident I had staged the play in Kaduna, Zaria, Lagos, Ibadan and Abeokuta without trouble. That was why I was shocked that the Jos Police took a different attitude.

However my arrest did me a good turn. It made me a hero in Northern Nigeria. Fans gathered round me and made voluntary subscriptions to pay for the services of two counsel, who defended me, and the court fine. I was left a handsome balance after paying for the expenses!

This wonderful generosity of the people on the Plateau inspired me to continue my tour of the Region. Unfortunately for me the Kano Police were not prepared to be outdone in the business of protecting His Majesty's subjects from the "bad" influences of Hubert Ogunde and His Concert Party. Just as I landed in Kano the Police called on me and warned me not to stage "Strike and Hunger" in the walled city.

When I first came into the show business I used to play with native drums. Most of the songs in my plays were in Yoruba. That was the position until I visited Ghana in 1948.

The journey to Ghana was a big failure. It was obvious why I failed. The Ghanaians could not understand the Yoruba dialect and that killed their interest in my plays.

I think I can claim that I brought Nigerian girls into music. When I started my band in 1950 I thought girls would be useful material—to attract boys! So I started teaching girls how to play the alto-saxophone.

The first girl I taught was Clementina, who later became my wife. I met her when she attended one of my shows in Ibadan, in 1946.

Clementina, who comes from my village Ososa, had come to Ibadan to spend her holidays. After seeing the shows, she moved up to me and said she wanted to join the party which was then composed of about thirty girls.

I took her on but it was not long when I found myself falling in love with her. Since we married in 1946, Clementina has been taking the leading roles in all my plays. We visited England together.

My failure in Ghana in 1948 was always in my mind. As every showman would, I was always planning to revisit Ghana and redeem my good name. The opportunity came in December 1950 when my band had reached a comparatively high standard.

It was the first time I took the band out of Lagos. On our way we stopped at Lome and played at a local club. After the show we were invited by Mr. Tonvenyadji, who owns a night club, to play at his club on New Year's eve. Mr. Tonvenyadji made such a fuss about Hubert Ogunde and His Girls from Nigeria and I am happy we did not let him down.

Nigerian parents don't encourage their children—especially girls—to take to the stage. Often the girls are willing—they find the stage exciting and charming—but their parents prevail on them to quit.

Once I had a brilliant girl in my party. I was paying her £15 a month. But she quit to take a job as a petrol station attendant on £3 a month! Her parents thought that was much more respectable job.

Certainly I could not continue to put up with this state of affairs. It was clearly ruining my business. I had to think how to arrest the situation.

The answer was to make it a family business where I would have complete control over the members.

Today members of the Ogunde Concert Party are nearly all from my family. Three of the girls are my wives; two are my relatives who have been married to the manager of the party and his assistant. The boys are members of my family.

My Struggles

I inherited my stage talent from my mother's parents. My grandfather was Babalawo (a diviner). He was versed in occultism and organized masquerade performances. Thus, I was initiated into many cults at an early age. I played truant in my school days running away from classes to join the masquerades. That was in the year 1931 and I was then fourteen years old, having been born in 1917 [1916] at Ososa, four miles to Ijebu Ode in the Western State of Nigeria.

My father, Mr. Jeremaiah [sic] Dehinbo Ogunde was an evangelist of the Baptist Church. He was among the first students of Baptist Seminary Ogbomosho. My mother, Eunice Owotusam Ogunde was also very devoted.

My father's missionary duties which took him from one town to the other made it impossible for me to complete my elementary school career at a station.

I completed my elementary school, which was the only education I had, in 1932 [1933], after attending four different schools. Saint John's School, Ososa [Baptist School Ife], was my first school and my last was Wasimi African School, Ijebu Ode after I had schooled at Baptist School, Ife and Saint Peters School, Faji, Lagos.

I became a wage earner in 1933 [1934] when I took to teaching. I was then earning the handsome sum of ten shillings a month. In those days, a policeman was an attractive sight; his well-ironed uniform and the authority he wielded gave the clarion call to many youths. I left the teaching field and joined the police force in 1940 [1941]. During my years with the force, I was staging dramas on part-time bases.

My first play was "Garden of Eden" in June 1933 [1944]. It was followed by "Africa and God," staged in September of the same year.

I quit the police force in 1946 [1945] and turned professional in the stage business. With a capital of £39 (₦18) which was all I could save, I bought some equipment. It was an uphill task gathering people to join my troupe. My parents thought it was sheer madness to allow their children take concert-acting as their profession. However, I managed to assemble the first troupe and presented the play "King Solomon". I toured many parts of the country to present this play and the reaction of the audience was favourable. My plays have been drawing sizable audiences since I began staging shows but the strength of the audience depends on the nature of the play being presented.

After the general strike of 1945, I staged a play "Strike and Hunger" which became a hit with the indigenous population while the colonial masters thought the play was inciting the people to riot. When I took the play to the Northern Region in 1946, I was arrested and prosecuted in Jos. The £200 [£125] fine imposed on me was paid by the Yoruba community in Jos, but my troupe was banned from performing in the North. I also received this type of treatment during the Western Nigeria crises when I staged the play "Yoruba Ronu." Most of my plays have been warmly received by the public but I regard as my hit plays "King Solomon," "Strike and Hunger," "Yoruba Ronu," and "Ayomo." I have also waxed many numbers in Yoruba language and these include *Orilonishe*, *Onijonimi*, *Eiyeire* and *Yeyemi*. Many of my records are still in great demand.

In June 1974, I shall be celebrating my thirty years on the stage. It has been a long way since June 1944 when I came out with my curtain raiser—"Garden of Eden." It has also been an interesting period. I have had the opportunity of making many friends and seeing many parts of the world. At the early stage of my profession, my wife and I toured Britain, France and Italy to get acquainted with the stage set-ups. My troupe was at the 1967 Canadian Expo. In 1958-69, the military government sponsored my troupe—forty in number—to Britain and the rest of Europe. We were well received and our performances were widely acclaimed by the British and world press.

I am now 56 years old. I am married to many wives and have many children. My two sons and three daughters are among my troupe while others are pursuing their calls in life. I am looking forward to the World Black Arts Festival and soon after that, I shall retire from the stage and retain only a supervisory role. Looking back to it now, I am very grateful to all Nigerians and foreigners who have made my struggles worthwhile.

Rotimi and Soyinka at Unife: A Newspaper Controversy

Theater history is beginning to emerge as an important new discipline at African universities. Master's theses and doctoral dissertations on aspects of local theater history have already been produced by scholars from Nigeria, Ghana, Cameroon, Tanzania, Malawi and several other countries with strong theatrical traditions. The first of these professionally trained theater historians did their advanced degrees abroad, but today an increasing number are completing their studies at home, investigating phenomena that can be researched more exhaustively in an indigenous setting. These pioneering young academics are recovering Africa's theatrical past.

One problem in carrying out such research is that of locating reliable documentary records. Even relatively recent events will be remembered by various witnesses differently, so the theater historian must make an effort to cross-check oral interviews by consulting written materials and other tangible records produced during the period under scrutiny. For a history of a stage company, for instance, he or she would have to examine printed programs, contemporary newspaper reviews, published interviews, and whatever photographs or films of performances might still survive. Some of these materials will be housed in convenient archives or held by individuals active in the company concerned; others will be lost or scattered and will have to be sought out by resorting to techniques reminiscent of those employed by Sherlock Holmes. It is entirely possible that vital records will elude even the most painstaking scholar simply because they appeared in media regarded as too ephemeral or too fragile for preservation; they may be remembered and talked about, but copies can no longer be found.

This is often the case with newspaper items that made a sensation in their day but were never systematically recorded, collected and archived. How does one get hold of such data? If there are no newspaper indexes to refer to and no well-stocked newspaper libraries within easy traveling distance, the researcher may be faced with the proverbial problem of hunting for a needle in a haystack—and a faraway haystack at that. It may be useful, therefore, for theater journals to reprint important documents that are now extremely rare or inaccessible to most researchers. As an example of what I have in mind, I am offering for reproduction here a set of interesting cuttings from several 1983 issues of the *Nigerian Tribune*, a newspaper published in Ibadan. Though these are relatively recent materials, the *Nigerian Tribune* is not held in many African newspaper collections, so the important theater debate stirred up in its pages a few years ago will be unknown and unavailable to the vast majority of scholars interested in contemporary Nigerian theater history.

The controversy focused on the University of Ife theater and on two distinguished Nigerian playwrights who had directed productions there: Ola Rotimi and Wole Soyinka. Rotimi, after returning from undergraduate and graduate theater studies in the United States in 1966, was attached briefly to the University of Ibadan before moving on to the University of Ife to take up an appointment as Director of the University Theatre, a position he held until 1977. Soyinka, based at the University of Lagos from 1965 to 1967 and held in detention from 1967 to 1969 during the Nigerian civil war, spent 1970 to 1975 in self-exile in Europe and Ghana. Upon returning to Nigeria, he accepted an appointment as Professor of Comparative Literature at the University of Ife and soon became involved in dramatic productions there. When Rotimi left, he took over as Head of the Theatre Arts program and Director of the University Theatre, positions he held until he opted to take early retirement in 1985. During their twenty years at Ife, these two talented directors, who also had become

Nigeria's pre-eminent playwrights, made the "Unife Theatre" into one of the most exciting centers of theatrical activity on the African continent.

Inevitably, people compared them—as playwrights, as directors, as men of the theater. Each had a compelling theatrical vision and a distinctive professional style. Each had a strong personality. And each had devoted backers and detractors who argued interminably about the respective merits and demerits of both. When one of the Soyinkaphiles ventured to publish in the *Nigerian Tribune* a brief account of the Unife Theatre that belittled Rotimi's achievements there, it was only natural that the Rotimites should respond. Indeed, the response came from Ola Rotimi himself, who offered a lengthy rebuttal in three installments. This prompted a "correction" from Soyinka, which in turn led to a series of rejoinders from both sides. The whole palaver is reprinted here, starting with the first salvo, which was fired on 12 February 1983 by Kole Omotoso, then a Lecturer in Arabic at the University of Ife and a good friend of Soyinka's:

UNIFE THEATRE

The University of Ife Theatre has always realized itself, in its more than ten years of existence, within a larger unit of the University of Ife. At its inception, it was part of the old Institute of African Studies and it expressed itself in the Ife Festival of the Arts. When in 1977 it was thought that an African university should be in its totality an institute of African Studies, and so the specific Institute of African Studies was dissolved to create four departments, the University of Ife Theatre became an arm of the new Department of Dramatic Arts. The process of this change and the trend of the continuity are complex and anyway need not be related here. Suffice it to say that the first part of the history of the theatre ends with Ola Rotimi's move to Port Harcourt and Wole Soyinka's assumption of responsibility for the theatre from 1977.

If there is need to give an example of the continuity in different dimensions, it is in the initial composition of the company, consisting as it did then, of enthusiastic amateurs, be they farmers or carpenters or school teachers and the guerrilla theatre activities.

The initial composition of the company was to help seal the relationship between the university and the town of Ile-Ife just as the guerrilla theatre takes instant theatre to the streets of the town and the open spaces of the university. If it has taken this long time to see the linkage and continuity, it is because the story of the theatre had been viewed from the perspective of the directors—the founding director, Ola Rotimi, and his successor, Wole Soyinka, instead of being viewed from the perspective of the theatre itself, as something growing, expanding, changing like all living organisms.

The University of Ife Theatre premiered all of Ola Rotimi's plays until his departure from the university in 1977. More than the experience of these premieres was the absorption by the company of a particularly rigid mode of production. Ola Rotimi has an epic hand in the dispersal of characters, props and set on the stage. He could get a hundred things going on the stage without one duplicating another. He was meticulous in working out for each person on stage the particularity of their movement on the stage.

This rigidity could be partly explained by the fact that many of those who were members of the company at the period he headed it were sometimes no better than enthusiastic green hands for whom things must be spelt out or else everything would spill out.

While Ola Rotimi produced the plays of other playwrights, using the University of Ife Theatre company, he never allowed any other play director to work with the company as long as he was heading it. Some of the plays of others which he directed himself include *The Family* by C. Ekiye and *The Curse* by Kole Omotoso. This attitude must have strengthened the rigidity of the company for those years he headed it. It is perhaps, in the spirit of this rigidity that Ola Rotimi was decided against having anything to do with the hall that later came to be known as Oduduwa Hall. He saw it as a monstrosity that could not respond to the handling of a director of plays, more so since the university authorities did not consult him in the planning of the hall. Perhaps because of his epic production style, the space most usually favoured by Ola Rotimi was and is the courtyard, preferably of split level rather than something that seems to give the impression of a proscenium.

When Wole Soyinka took over in 1977, he saw no reason why attempts should not be made to rescue what could be rescued from what the Italian builders were doing. He therefore went ahead and cooperated with them, made suggestions and virtually took over the hall on behalf of the University of Ife Theatre. This takeover and use of Oduduwa Hall, along with the Pit Theatre located in the African Studies buildings, meant the virtual abandonment of the building at Arubidi in the town of Ife where Ola Rotimi used to produce his plays. At Arubidi, the theatre was visible and seen to be doing things whereas in Oduduwa Hall and in the Pit Theatre the public was shut out. Space, therefore, and attitude to space played a part in that complex process of making change and producing continuity within the University of Ife Theatre.

Finally, the directorial approach of Wole Soyinka is different from that of Ola Rotimi. Soyinka works with both the script and the actor, changing the lines and the movements as both come to share a relationship of understanding and identification. One invariably remembers the performances of Soyinka's plays, those which he directed himself, by the characters as interpreted by actors and actresses to the extent that the names of such roles tend to stick to those who played them at the first performance. This type of directorial approach expects much from the individual actor and actress. When we remember the medley composition of the company under Ola Rotimi and the different levels of formal education and theatre experience, it was certain that the theatre which Soyinka took over would not be adequate for his purposes.

For quite some time since 1977, Soyinka has used students, members of staff, as well as members of the University of Ife Theatre in his productions. This could be only a temporary solution. With the establishment of the Department of Dramatic Arts, a slow process of training for the members of the company began through the one-year certificate programme in Dramatic Arts. Along with this programme for those who were thought capable of benefiting from the training went the re-deployment or outright dismissal of those who could not cope with the new requirements.

While all these complex moves were taking place, the University of Ife Theatre continued to premiere the plays of Wole Soyinka as well as other playwrights.

The result of the training, of the diversified production styles, the inculcation of confidence in each actor and actress is paying off now and it is bound to increase in the future. The University of Ife Theatre began as a pioneering experiment, being first of its type to be attached to a university in Nigeria. The theatre has not abandoned that pioneering spirit. It has come a short way to be such a formidable unit which will go a long way in the history of theatre performance in Nigeria.

Rotimi, stung by some of these assertions, tried to put the record straight in a three-part reply carried in the *Nigerian Tribune* on March 19th, 23rd and 26th:

(1) Since my departure from Ife I've been silent. Resolutely silent because I wanted time to think—think of how I could be far more relevant, more relevant to this nation through my calling.

Because I yearn for fewer distractions, but seem to find this ideal permanently elusive, I have become more conscious of the value of time. I must admit, too, that I'm inclined to being more cynical of forums that tend to further claim what little time I may have for my own. In this respect, I have refrained from taking up membership of organizations, even of such as the Association of Nigerian Authors, or what have you. I've been keeping myself to myself—only scurrying out on occasional sallies with a new work or other, and retreating quickly to my enshackled condition with its everlasting administrative usurpation of my longing to be left alone to just teach, research, write, publish and produce.

Impotent in my toothy dependence on that monthly salary— which, I hear, Vice President Ekwueme and Governor Aper Aku are even now threatening to halve in the name of cure for our ravished economy—I find my dilemma growing more disconcerting in its mind-numbing details. The greater reason for wanting to keep myself to myself, and fetishly protect my time and peace.

But it seems I can't even have that peace. Dr. Kole Omotoso's article in the *Nigerian Tribune* of Saturday, February 12, 1983, for instance, is a clear case of what, in pidgin, we describe as "trouble de sleep, monkey go wake am!"

Before I set to, I have this one and only regret to express. Wole Soyinka's name has been invoked—for reasons best known to Dr. Omotoso—into the said article in a manner which I consider most unfortunate. My relationship with Wole Soyinka (for those who might want to know) has been most cordial. Indeed, brotherly, I would say.

Well, there was a time—just before I left Ife University—when certain persons in high places in that institution would have succeeded in causing friction between us. I must say that, in the height of those ominous moments, it was Wole himself who took the initiative of advising that, no matter the provocations, we both must try to save our relationship from external abuse.

Since my departure from Ife, Wole has, in a number of ways, made me feel that his plea for mutuality between us, was sincere. I would like to think that he, too, has had cause to confirm my openness towards him.

Sadly, however, it would seem that, for reasons best known to them, some persons in the same Unife Department of Dramatic Arts are becoming dizzy with a free-wheeling sense of history to a degree that is clearly insidious.

Since I know something about the Unife Theatre that has been the focus of a spate of press publications in recent times, and since my name was particularly juggled with in Dr. Omotoso's own write-up, I owe it to history to correct some of the patently groveling outpourings. So now...

Essentially, the publication by Dr. Omotoso set out to compare the character of Ife University Theatre under my directorship (i.e., 1966 to 1977), with what it is now under a different management of which he happens to be a part. Fair enough. And this is not my gripe.

Comparative studies are normal in scholarship to which Dr. Omotoso and I make claim. My gripe is simply that Dr. Omotoso has treated this norm with amazing levity, glorifying trivialities and celebrating untruths. This, to me, is most dangerous because the Doctor, like me, is a teacher—a dispenser of knowledge to trusting minds. It is dangerous to possess the capacity for feeding high-protein trash to such trusting minds, just because one prefers the ease that goes with lazy research.

To start with, some fundamental corrections are necessary, at this point. The learned writer claimed that "the Institute of African Studies at Unife was dissolved in 1977 to create FOUR Departments..." Misinformation! The Institute of African Studies was not dissolved in 1977, but in 1975. Second. The Departments that emerged from that dissolution were not FOUR, but two, namely: Music and Dramatic Arts.

It is probable that Dr. Omotoso also had the Department of Fine Arts as well as the Department of African Languages and Literatures in mind in conclusion on FOUR departmental outgrowths. But the truth is, the sections of Fine Arts and African Languages and Literatures evolved from the Institute to become a degree-awarding Department as far back as in 1973 and '74, respectively. Not '77. Anyway, let that pass.

Other points. I don't know how Dr. Omotoso got the idea that I did not want to co-operate with the "Italian" builders who constructed Oduduwa Hall. Nor can I fathom the basis of his concluding that it was Soyinka who redeemed that majestic theatre building from neglect. To begin with, I did undertake the planning of Oduduwa Hall with the architects. But, as is usually the case with such multi-purpose ventures, there came a stage where technocracy took over, and the artist's interests had to tolerate other needs. Even so, I never was going to abandon Oduduwa Hall. As a matter of fact, we did stage *Kurunmi* in the Oduduwa Hall amphitheatre in 1974 or thereabout.

The true position was this. With four other venues (including the Pit) for play-production at my disposal on Ife University campus, and another one downtown Ife, I had no real urgency for the inner theatre of Oduduwa Hall. The open air allure of traditional African theatre was my preference. All the venues, excepting the inner hall of Oduduwa, had that allure—as Dr. Omotoso himself seemed to have observed.

Be that as it may, there was yet another reason why I wasn't too much in a rush to use the inner Oduduwa Hall. It was that railing. I can't remember noticing it in the initial designs I planned with the architects. But, there it was in the building upon completion. That railing. That 20-odd inches high, galvanized pipe barrier on the stage-floor separating actors from spectators. I had meant to quietly dismantle that metallic apartheid someday, so that both actors and audience could flow into one. I never got round to that. The railing is still there—as cheerfully redundant as ever!

All told, there were no major modifications that the Hall required after it was built. Nothing structural, at any rate. And contrary to Dr. Omotoso's hint, I don't think Wole Soyinka undertook a crucial "rescue" work on the Hall either. The changes I recall noticing being made were on the exterior decoration of the Hall. Facade touches mainly in which white emulsion sweeps replaced the original, ill-matching purple on the same abstract designs. That's all. Functionally, rather scant to warrant chronicling.

But then, to a hustler in the field, such flimsies too, must count as epochal index to contrastive studies in Theatre History. Anyway, now to other matters in that publication.

Dr. Omotoso argues that the actors whom the present managers of Unife Theatre inherited from me suffered from a major handicap. He diagnoses this as a certain "rigidity" in their acting habit. He then goes on to ascribe the cause of that "rigidity" to the monopoly I had, as artistic director, over the actors throughout my stay at Ife.

Coming from someone like Dr. Omotoso who was one of the more regular visitors to the old Unife Theatre at work, this statement is plain wicked. Kole Omotoso knew that I never monopolized the handling of those actors. With me from 1968 to 1977 when I left Ife, were two other senior academics who were also full-time artistic directors of the group. They were Dr. Akin Euba and Miss Peggy Harper. There was yet another equally able colleague—from 1970 to 1972/73—Dr. Sam Akpabot. We all worked with the group at will.

A more seasoned coterie of artistic directors is yet to be found on this land. Which speaks more for the vision and mature sense of mission of Professor Hezekiah Oluwasanmi—the second Vice-Chancellor of the University that flaunts "Learning and Culture" as its motto.

Granted, Akin Euba and Sam Akpabot are specialists in music. Nonetheless, they both also worked with the group in idioms as markedly theatrical as mine. They both directed the actors in musical dramas. For instance, Akin Euba, assisted by Peggy Harper, handled the actors in such works as *Chaka* and *Obaluaye*; and Sam Akpabot, in his own *Jaja of Opobo*.

The crucial point here is that Akin Euba and Sam Akpabot also handled those actors in exploring the realms of acting, movement and directing. More can be said of the involvement of Peggy Harper whose special area is choreography and movement.

Dr. Omotoso's picture reducing those actors to histrionic fossils is, therefore, hardly borne out by the dynamics of the actors' circumstances during my years with them. Let's examine the circumstances further.

For the sake of argument, let's even believe that no one else but me, handled the actors to the extent in which their acting became stereotyped.

To start with, Dr. Omotoso graciously concedes in his article that I did stage the plays of other authors. Not just my work. He mentions *The Family* by Comish Ekiye. A modern, middle-class, social drama. He also cites his own *The Curse*. But what the learned Doctor fails to tell the reader—as expected of a true theatre scholar—is whether the acting and directing styles for staging my more traditional *The Gods...* or *Kurunmi*, are also the same for *The Family*, or for his own allegorical fantasy, *The Curse*.

Certainly, Omotoso knows that the genre, time-setting, and cultural matrix of a play do determine acting style as much as directing approach. Elementary theatre knowledge, this. Well, then, how can he talk of "rigidity" in acting response, when the same actors, as he himself tells us, were exposed to plays of intrinsically varied acting and directing styles? Confusion.

(2) If Dr. Omotoso is implying that the old Unife actors were used to my kind of artistic vibrations, one would agree with him, even though he would be saying nothing new. You can't work with another human being—even an animal—let alone a corporate body of beings, and not expect some degree of mutuality in sensory tuning. Even then, transferred to new hands, what such actors require is a period of re-orientation in which the 'new-comer' director must take the lead, inspiring faith and confidence. If no director is prepared to go through this strain, it is unfair to blame 'rigidity' on the actors.

Like the fellow who came from Ibadan, eager to work with the group soon after I left Ife. He plunged straight into business, then soon realized he couldn't cope, gave up in a matter of days, and scuttled back to Ibadan, self-righteously wondering how anyone could achieve things with those kinds of actors! But the answer is simple. Patience. The trouble is, most so-called Nigerian theatre directors bustle forth, wanting to USE actors. This is wrong. A good director does not USE actors. He works with and shapes them.

Or as Goethe puts it, he "advance(s) them in their art." Acutely true in our developing Nigeria.

Another point. The Doctor attributes what he calls "rigidity" of the actors they inherited from me to yet another factor. This is that I never allowed any theatre director from outside to work with the group. What logic! Stanislavsky must be squirming with guilt in his grave for having dominated the Moscow Art Theatre with his own directing vision! So must be Goethe and his monolithic presence over Germany's Weimar Theatre; Laura Keene and America's Chestnut Theatre.

Perhaps I'm invoking the ghosts of distant cultures. Let's be homebound then. Directors Ogunde, Baba Sala, your actors are doomed to "rigidity", they say, unless you make way now for all comers.

Anyway, back to the point. Perhaps the questions should be: Did any outside director come forward, offering to work with the Unife Theatre, in my time, and was put off? To my recollection, no one approached us. Which was just as well, anyhow. As far as I know, there were only two theatre practitioners in Nigeria at that time who I could have welcomed to handle that Unife group in dramatic production. Only two persons whose knowledge of theatre directing I trusted. Unfortunately, they never approached us.

Of course, quite a number of people think they know what directing is all about. Fine. Everyone is entitled to private delusions. But those who really know about directing, do appreciate the fact that it is a science that goes beyond mere transmission of content through actors in a series of configurations on an action-space. Thank goodness, "outsiders" who ogle at the director's science didn't venture to embarrass themselves by offering to work with the Unife actors in my time. That theatre had no room for dilettantes! More especially when such dilettantes think that a Ph.D. dissertation on some tangential work in drama submitted for, say a degree in Arabic or French studies, does qualify them for work with actors who take the business of acting as their life! No way.

In his desperation to establish a base whereon to highlight—if prematurely—the qualities of the Unife Theatre under the new management, in contrast to the Old theatre, the Doctor describes the latter as "consisting...of enthusiastic amateurs...farmers, carpenters...school teachers."

The hint of educational lapse is implicit in the Doctor's spotlight on the more artisan background of the actors in the old theatre. The hint is deliberate. It serves the biased intentions of the Doctor, to the extent that the description is lopsided. In the old theatre were carpenters, bicycle-repairers, farmers, teachers, painters, tailors—and their wives too! True. But in addition to, and working as actors or stagehands in close partnership with them, were University staff of equally assorted background. Professor Michael Crowder (Historian), Professor H.L. Moody (English), Dr. Adebona (Lecturer in Botany), Femi Robinson (Chemical Technologist), Margaret Folarin (Lecturer in English), Leke Owolabi (Senior Accountant), Dr. George Reid (Lecturer in Philosophy) and more.

I am using the adjective 'old' pointedly, because there seems to be a piteously strenuous effort by persons of the Omotoso ilk to draw a red line between everything that the Ife Theatre was, up till 1977 when I left, and the wonders that the Omotosos proclaim to be happening to it ever since.

As far as I am concerned, the University of Ife Theatre, in my time, endeavoured to create a unity between the University and the Nigerian people, though art. We called that policy "integration of town and gown." I strongly believe that the University of Ife Theatre today is still capable of fostering that aim. And I also believe that it is possible, quite possible for Nigerians to advance a cause without first effacing the identity of the precedents that had nurtured that cause.

Dr. Omotoso's insular focus on farmers and carpenters cannot but be deliberate, as it provides the desired leverage for the learned doctor's innuendo on the mental inadequacy of those actors whom he ascribes to the "old" Ife Theatre.

His description also sees them as "enthusiastic amateurs." Clearly, Dr. Omotoso's idea of amateurism is at variance with the dictionary acceptation of that word. Let's analyze his inference. Among my early actors were people like Muraina Oyelami and Tunji Buraimoh, and Tijani Mayakiri. They had been full-time actors under the late Duro Ladipo, before coming to me at Ife. There was also Gboyega Ajayi, former leading actor in the Adejobi Theatre Group. Certainly, Dr. Omotoso is not implying that the Adejobi Theatre or Duro Ladipo Theatre is an amateur group—if he is being sincere about his claim to knowledge of Nigerian Theatre History.

When the Murainas and the Mayakiris, and the Gboyega Ajayis and the Ogundepos and the Ayantunji Amoos and the Peter Badejos came to assist in my search for contact with our artistic roots, they were already master-performers in their own right. They joined the University of Ife Theatre at its inception (then called Ori Olokun Players) and received monthly stipend. What was so amateurish in the make-up of the old group, that doesn't exist in the new?

In another paragraph of that publication, the Omotosos would have the world believe also that involvement of students is one salient feature of the composition of the present Unife Theatre. That's a lot of baloney, as the Americans say! At the same time that carpenters were bustling with farmers and me in the old Unife Theatre, University students were also an integral part of that theatre's acting personnel.

The students at that time included Bode Sowande (now a lecturer at Ibadan University), Tony Obilade (also now a lecturer at Ibadan University), Akin Sofoluwe (the Agricultural Engineering student, who was the first Kurunmi), Seinde Arigbede (then a medical student at the University of Ibadan). Again the list could go on, and on. Yinka Okeowo—now NFA Secretary—in his student days, was the first Ifa Priest in *Ovonramwen Nogbaisi*; Ade Onigbinde—now NFA Chief Football Coach—was one of the early Balogun Ibikunles in *Kurunmi*. The Sholu sisters—both lawyers now. Mrs. Yinka Anjorin. Where does one end?

To talk less of notable outsiders like Segun Akinbola, who resigned his post of Senior Executive Producer at NTV-Lagos, to work full-time with the group, satisfied to earn a lower salary because of his belief in the philosophy and artistic orientation of that kind of theatre.

True, the "students" referred to above, were not formally enrolled in Departments of Dramatic Arts. But our talk is not on Theatre Historians, or Theatre Analysts, but on acting and actors. Talent then, not paper qualification, must be the crucial measure here. Drama schools do not implant talent in students. They only stimulate and discipline talent in the perfection of skill. With the right teachers helping, of course! The deduction is that, to be a good actor, you either have IT (i.e., talent) or you don't. And with that basic stuff called talent, the rest is up to a sensitive director to educe the desired skill from it.

That those students in the old Theatre played their roles in ways that have made memorable impression throughout Nigeria, Ghana, in France and in Germany in the mid-sixties and seventies, is a testimony of their ability to match any Drama School snippet on the brass-tacks of acting. Granted, the Drama School student of Acting would excel when it comes to citing the theories of acting from Stanislavskian technique across to Agnes de Mille's; would certainly excel in mouthing Aristotelian unities—if irrelevantly! But in the matter of down-to-earth, acting know-how, the type that spirals organically from felt sensations within, to kinetic realizations, without? Let's not kid ourselves.

A classic story comes to mind here. The name Faye Dunaway is quite familiar to the film fan in Nigeria. For those who might not know, well, Faye Dunaway is one of America's top film actresses living today. See *Chinatown*, *Eva Peron*, etc. Of course, that also means that Faye Dunaway is a millionairess. I saw a coverage on her in *Time Magazine* a few years back, saw her lolling uncaringly by a personal swimming pool which I'm sure costs as much as would pay the salaries of all the staff in Ife and Port Harcourt put together! Austerity or no austerity!

Well, actress Faye Dunaway was my classmate at Boston University's School of Fine and Applied Arts. I was studying playwriting and directing then. Faye was doing straight acting. Both of us, undergraduates, acted in class scenes together. All of a sudden, with an extra year to go for the Bachelor's degree, Faye said she was quitting—going to New York; just quitting, heading West—California, anywhere. She said all she wanted was a chance to get her teeth fully into the real thing: acting. She quit.

We all shook our heads, good kids, and went ahead, piously filing our applications to continue studies at graduate level. I landed in Yale, attracted by the John Gassners and Alois Naglers—big names in the study of Theatre History and Dramatic Literature. Returned home three years later. Loyal Nigerian! Now Diane Schultz.

Diane Schultz was one of the brightest at Boston. Like Faye, she too was studying acting. Extremely bright in the theories. But Diane Schultz had no acting 'umph', let's face it. Anyway, Diane too went straight to do graduate work. She is now a top-ranking academic in one of America's universities. Teaches Theatre History which, I'm sure, is being updated to include contemporary American Theatre History.

This in turn means that, as one of the queen bees who make the American theatre scene tick today, Faye Dunaway is being studied in Diane Schultz's seminars. So much for the fallacy about Dramatic Schools as automatic instillers of acting talent.

(3) In further groping for distinctions between the present Unife Theatre and the old, Dr. Omotoso makes some comparative passes between my directing style and that of Wole Soyinka. He concludes that members of the old Theatre couldn't cope with the requirements of Soyinka's directing approach which, as he puts it, "expects much from the individual actor and actress." And what is the singular mark of Soyinka's directing regimen? Dr. Omotoso explains that "Soyinka works with both the script and the actor, changing the lines and the movements as both come to share a relationship of understanding and identification."

Again the man has said nothing. Just another effluence of inanities, as far as knowledge of theatre theory and practice goes. I'll prove this later. For now, let me say that if this, indeed, was really the test applied in re-deploying and dismissing some of the old actors who, as we are told, "could not cope", then one wonders whether Dr. Omotoso's revelation gives credit to Wole Soyinka himself for adopting that kind of narrow test. Or should we now say that, this explains why, for instance, someone like Ayan Amao—

the superlative bata-drummer of the old theatre got "re-deployed" from the position of bata-drummer, to being a bartender at Oduduwa Hall?

Well, like the true artist that he is, good old Ayan Amao had his pride. He rejected that gracious "re-deployment" (or was it humiliation?), grabbed his bata-drum one morning, and headed South-West for Lagos where the University of Lagos quickly recruited his drumming expertise into its Centre for Cultural Studies. Some price we pay in Nigeria, in the name of "polish by the script"!

Back to the argument. As a criterion for testing the competence of performers in a group that strives to exemplify contemporary African theatre with roots in content, music, movement, etc., the insular focus on actors' response to script simply doesn't make sense.

However, this is not to say that there is no merit in "working with both script and actors, changing lines and movement..." Of course there is. Now, here is the rub: the business of "working with both script and actor etc." is a common chore in play-directing. Not an innovation. Certainly not a discovery! What else is a play director supposed to be doing with a script under his nose and actors before his eyes?

One doesn't have to look far, to know that the practice of "working with both script and actors, changing lines and movement etc. etc. etc." is a directing convention that dates deep into theatre history. What, for instance, does the learned Doctor think 16th Century theatre was demonstrating through the opening passages in Act III, Scene ii of Shakespeare's *Hamlet*?

For Dr. Omotoso to have displayed "working with both script and the actors bla-bla-bla," as a distinction of the Soyinkaesque directing acumen, is simply laughable in its nothingness. It's like saying Sunny Ade's sound is different from Victor Uwaifo's in that Sunny uses the guitar and conga drums! What does Victor use? This is not even lazy research. It is no research at all. The difference between Peugeot and Datsun is that Peugeot uses petrol and is meant to cover distances. Some distinction!

Certainly the learned Doctor can do better than that, in probing what really are the precise trademarks of Soyinka's or any other practitioner's craftsmanship in play-directing.

If it appears that I am being too hard on Dr. Omotoso, it is because this is not the first time I have had to draw his attention to the need for proper research before submitting work of informative value for publication. The first time was in 1977. Then, my communication to him was done in a private letter. It would seem that, six years after, the fellow is yet to appreciate the essence of research in addressing a subject of educational purport.

In a sense, one doesn't blame him. About time our real theatre historians and analysts—the Adedejis, and the Ogunbas and the Ogunbiyis—started looking into the dynamics of play production in our land. We've just about had our surfeit of the customary recycling of Western ideas on Brechtian techniques and Stanislavskian method into our students' skulls. Such fixations only serve to further nurture the kind of mulish commentaries on Nigerian theatre practice which one has been encountering here and there.

The English Departments may continue their monocled preoccupation with text if they like. But the theatre analyst/historian must begin to sit beside and watch how the Soyinkas and the Kalu Ukas, and the Adelugbas and the Zulu Sofolas and the Otis and the Maddys and the Ogundes grapple with their visions in directing. Essential to such investigation is the question as to whether these visions are aiming at something new, something relevant to African cultural expositions.

To start winding up, there is a point for which one must thank Dr. Omotoso. He did admit that (I quote) "the University of Ife Theatre began as a pioneering experiment, being first of its type to be attached to a university in Nigeria. The Theatre has not abandoned that pioneering spirit." (unquote). Amen. This much is heartening. And one is assuming, of course, that the "pioneering spirit" of which we are being reassured is that of commitment to a sustained communing with the people inside and outside the natty walls of our university campuses, through the medium of institutional theatre.

This is where the news that the new Unife Theatre would soon be going out on such missions—as of old—is most heartening.

Especially, in these times when austerity and FEDECO and sudden fires and surprise arrests are most unworthily claiming our minds.

The only thing though, if one may proffer some advice, is this: drama (for it to get to and be part of, the people) means and takes a lot of endurance. Running an itinerant theatre in an institutional setting, whether in a university or in a State Arts Council, is perhaps one of the most trying of theatre experiences. A fundamental reason is that those centres lack that secret which helps to sustain cohesion among theatre members, and which in turn ensures the kind of longevity which groups like Ogunde and Alawada theatres enjoy.

This central secret is the family unit, acting as the hub of a theatre's organization and practice. Institutions can still evolve a viable substitute for the family unit, through other patterns of personnel organization and group commitment to shared concerns. The ten-year life span (1967-77) of the old Unife Theatre has shown that ideas in that regard are workable.

This is not the place for details, but suffice to say that the old Unife Theatre's lifespan was insured on four principles, the knowledge of which I'd be most willing to share with whoever is so interested. Unfortunately in Nigeria, people don't seem to want to ask questions about the past with a view to improving on necessary points of departure. Rather, new builders prefer to destroy the past in an unnecessary drive for absolute credit.

The result is usually that the new building—not having benefited from an understanding of the contours of the land or the texture of materials—gets stunted at the DPC level. Like the Unibadan Traveling Theatre and its still sputtering efforts to move, after over two years of noisy proclamations about intentions of reaching out to the people.

Anyway, better luck to the new Unife Theatre. In this task, my friend, Wole, will certainly need the help of his colleagues—the Omotosos and the Ogunbiyis who must try to see their function as not dominant only in the proclamation of intentions from the rooftops of the *Nigerian Tribune* and the mountaintops of the *National Concord*.

Drama, as we know, derives from the Greek word Dran, which means 'doing". And when the doing actually gets going, pray, the theatre managers should not preempt the Nigerian public of their right to be ultimate judges of the drama they see, either. Things get rather incestuous when the very doers of the drama also arrogate to themselves the role of public interpreters.

Let's leave the self-advertising game to the Obeyas trying to tell Nigerians "what to think" about Mercedes Benz or no Mercedes Benz deals. After all, Plato may be right in maintaining that those who "produce" may know less about the value of the matter produced than those who "use" it. That could be true in Nigeria too. If only we would give it a try!

Three weeks later, on April 16th, Wole Soyinka offered some conciliatory remarks as well as "a correction":

Ola Rotimi's three-part series on Unife Theatre must have saddened many readers—they certainly had that effect on me. I intend to stay out of the controversy—apart, of course, from being cast willy-nilly, as a passive principal. Nevertheless I feel compelled, solely for the sake of the practicalities of theatre, to correct one erroneous understanding of Professor Ola Rotimi, obviously drawn from my "redeployment" of one musician, Ayantunji Amoo. I do not want the public to be left with the incorrect notion that traditional artistes have been given the boot in favour of "academic" artistes, any more than I would like bartenders to feel that their profession is looked down upon, and used as a dump for putting old theatre nags to grass.

The drummer in question was not "redeployed." I actually dispensed with his services, which were no longer required. The responsibility of the Artistic Director of a company with limited resources is to balance the various expertise within the company, not make it top-heavy in any one direction. Amoo was not the only casualty. At present we have three first-class drummers with the company, one of whom is illiterate in conventional language. But the language which he does speak—the language of dundun, gangan, etc.— is the language we need in the theatre. He is also disciplined, does not fall asleep during rehearsals and does not come late to performances—so he fits into the company. I do not know if he is an inferior or superior artiste to Ayantunji but he is more than adequate for our dramatic needs.

Amoo was re-employed by Oduduwa Hall as a barman some time afterwards and this was only as a result of passionate pleading by the late Ayansola who was Amoo's mentor and patron. Ayansola said, "Listen, you are punishing me, not him. The responsibility for him and his family will fall on me if you leave him jobless." So I gave him a job as a barman in Oduduwa Hall with a promise to recall him if the fortunes of the company improved to such an extent that I could afford to give him another chance. There are no hard feelings between Amoo and myself; he has been here to say hello to me a couple of times since he left for Lagos.

Even more to the point, I do not see redeployment as a barman, particularly when the bar is an integral part of the entire theatre organisation, as a humiliation. One lesson which I try to impress on all members of the company, including students, is that no activity connected with the theatre is beneath them. If a bar is required to make the theatre pay its way, then the artistes in that company must be prepared to serve drinks, mop the floor and flush the slop. I took over the bar myself during the performances of *Dream on Monkey Mountain*, directed by Carroll Dawes, a role into which I slipped naturally because of my post-graduate education as a barman-cum-bouncer, among other jobs. An excellent artist here whose painting decorates my wall runs a bakery on the side. Seven "academic" artistes bit the dust in my last few months as Head of Department, and a very well-known Visiting Artiste who has worked with me off and on since the early sixties was recently given a two-month suspension by the new Head of Department for unprofessional conduct. If he had asked for a job as barman in Oduduwa Hall during his suspension, I would have done my best to accommodate him.

Famous actors and artistes all over the world, no matter their country's ideological policy towards the arts, take on the most bizarre assortment of jobs during "laying off" or slack seasons. There are indeed restaurants and bars which specialise in part-time vacancies for theatre artistes—this is the sort of tradition which we have tried to emulate here by our special symbiotic relationship with Oduduwa Hall, a relationship which, incidentally, gives our Bursar sleepless nights and some dons here bouts of apoplexy.

There are far too many other errors of thinking and reading of facts in what Ola has written so let me just end by advising that, all in all, it is safer to leave the internal organisation—which includes matters of discipline—of any theatre company to the on-the-spot leadership of the company, as events often wear deceptive looks— rather like the profession of acting itself. I can only hope that the present dust settles down quickly so we can get back to the normal business of collaborating on creative projects.

I wish to recall Ola to the fact that when Unife theatre acquired its video recording equipment three years ago, our first project was to bring him back for a spell so that he could recreate his former triumphs and put them on tape. Unfortunately, he had already completed plans to go to the U.S. on sabbatical and the project was shelved. Now, this was not just a personal decision by me but the collective goal of the department which embraced the idea enthusiastically. Surely, this is a far more accurate gauge of the attitude of staff here to Ola Rotimi's work, than any critical incidentals in an essay by a colleague. Other collaborations since his departure should be placed at the forefront of Ola's assessment of the genuineness of appreciation of his work both by his former actors and his erstwhile colleagues. Like all genuine appreciation, it is not an uncritical one, and I wish Ola would try to read genuine critical interest where now he appears to read nothing but bad faith.

To this Rotimi responded on April 27th with a statement he called "My Last Word":

It is convenient for Professor Wole Soyinka to excuse the misrepresentations in Dr. Omotoso's article breezily as "critical incidentals." To me, and I should think, to the Nigerian public at large, among whom are Theatre/Literature students, accuracy of research data is no matter for cavalier scoffing.

This thinking has nothing to do with testiness to critical assessment, either. It is a matter of not playing dumb in the face of mass misguidance against which one happens to have a chance to react. Anyhow, times change. But yesterday, it was Wole Soyinka in a stout fight against what, to him, were misconceptions and misrepresentations in Neo-Tarzanism: The Poetics of Pseudo-

Tradition. Today, my own reaction to a similar 'outrage' has become much ado over "critical incidentals."

Just as baffling is Wole's claim in the opening paragraph of his contribution. He says: "Ola Rotimi's three-part series on Unife Theatre must have saddened many readers..." It is indeed, tragic, if readers can be saddened at my calling a teacher who trivializes facts to order. The only consolation then seems to be that a number of students and staff of the very Ife University have since thanked me for finding the time to put an aspect of their history in proper perspective. The results of an opinion poll as to which side enjoys the greater sympathy, would mean nothing to me, since my objective in this debate was neither to gladden or sadden hearts, in the first place.

Now to the Ayan Amao matter which evoked so much sermonizing on the dignity of labour. So, discipline also had to do with that case. Fine. But why wasn't that intimated before? Instead, the aptitude for script-work was emblazoned on the original publication as the measure whereby some of the old Unife actors were knocked out. That was the 'cue line' given. I only reacted to it and deduced that, in such circumstances, illiterate artistes like the bata-drum expert Ayan stood small chance. The latest revelation only serves to prove my contention that the original dish on the Unife Theatre was not painstakingly prepared. Too many vexatious flakes of raw onion and unground egusi.

Of course, I'm all for discipline. More poignantly, discipline imposed not only on the rank and file, but also one modeled on the moral and manual leadership of the bosses themselves. That is one of the secrets of the 10-year longevity of the Old Unife Theatre.

One would have expected Wole, if he meant his contribution to be meaningful, to call staff-member Omotoso and tell him candidly that his article had some gaffes. Which done, if Wole had anything to say to me, he knew how to get in touch. We do correspond from time to time. But then, the question could be asked: why must Wole contact me? After all, did I contact Dr. Omotoso before bearing down on him? The answer is: yes, I did. As stated in my rejoinder, I had privately cautioned him on his approach to facts in another article: In 1977.

This time around, not only did he repeat the same tendency, but also decided to publish the result in a national newspaper. Not stopping there, he further went ahead—with the blessing of his Department, I now have reason to believe—to publish the stuff again in a pamphlet. Hundreds of copies of that pamphlet were churned out, carted along on a tour, and distributed North, South, East and West of the Federation as part of the programme notes for a play. The "critical incidentals" and all—in the name of comparative study which really was more like a narcissistic rhapsody played in vitiation of someone else's past.

Having, I suppose, made my points clear, well, I agree. We should let the dust over this matter settle quickly. The dust needn't have eddied in the first place—with a little consideration for the consequences of biased chronicling.

Kole Omotoso, whose newspaper article had kicked off the whole controversy, came back on June 1st with a brief rejoinder entitled "On Unife Theatre: Ola Rotimi's Last But Not Lasting Word":

All I wish to do in this response to Rotimi's long reaction to my short piece on the Unife Theatre is to re-iterate the facts that I mentioned in that piece, to mention a few others about Ola Rotimi's work and to elaborate on one particular issue.

It is a fact that Ola Rotimi did not permit any other director to direct the Unife Theatre while he ran it. It is a fact that Ola Rotimi's style of directing is dictatorial and there is nothing strange about this. Different directors have their different styles of directing. It is a fact that the Unife Theatre has grown beyond what Ola Rotimi left behind, whether he likes it or not. Some of the people he used to summon with whistles now direct their own productions and manage productions.

Other facts that can be asserted about Ola Rotimi's work include his conservative and backward historical attitude in his historical plays. There is also the unimaginative use of specific foreign nationals to play themselves in his plays. Here the Unife Theatre had gone beyond him. In productions such as *The Biko Inquest*, *Death and the King's Horseman*, and *Requiem for a Futurologist*, we have used black people, Africans, to play the roles of South

African Boers, British DO's and Indian loonies where Ola Rotimi would have gone searching for such nationals. The performance of these black people in these roles has been convincing and successful.

Ola Rotimi's production of my play, *The Curse*, for which he would expect my eternal gratitude, demonstrates his static sense of space on the stage. Against my advice, the cages were made of heavy iron and made stationary, instead of being mobile and light. This play was also produced more successfully by Dexter Lyndersay.

Some time in 1975, I was approached by a European theatre journal to do an article on adaptations of Sophocles' *Oedipus Rex* in different cultures of the Third World. I picked on two Arab playwrights—Tawfiq al-Hakim and Ali Ahmad Kathir, one Egyptian, the other from the Hadramaut—and one African playwright, Ola Rotimi. All these three playwrights have attempted to adapt the story of Oedipus into their cultures. In the case of the Arab-Muslim playwrights, one could see the influence and hand of their culture and religion on the situation of the Greek king.

But this is not so in the case of Ola Rotimi's *The Gods Are Not to Blame*. What Ola Rotimi has done is to simply transfer the story of King Oedipus to Yorubaland with Yoruba names without permitting Yoruba culture to influence his adaptation. In reading the original and Ola Rotimi's adaptation, one finds that but for the names there is no difference. One particularly major problem is that Yoruba gods are not as implacable as the Greek gods. Something would have to have been done to avert the horror of a man killing his father and marrying his mother. Ola told me that some Yoruba lady with royal connections in one of the Yoruba ruling houses had told him of a similar incident in Yorubaland. I said I would like to know this lady and source of her information. That information is still to be provided.

The other issue I mentioned in that article is the fact that Ola Rotimi's language trips when he moves from Yoruba to English, which statement he did not like. He has since produced a Yoruba version of *Kurunmi* which he insisted we should do instead of the English version.

It is to be noted that I am not the only one to have made these points about Ola Rotimi's work. And if I were to state now that Ola Rotimi's latest play *If* seems to take after *Moon on a Rainbow Shawl* (1958) by the Trinidadian (West Indian) playwright, Errol John, Ola Rotimi would want to know how I got to know of Caribbean playwrights when all I studied was Arabic!

As for Ola Rotimi's abuse of me in his articles, as well as in a personal note to Dr. Yemi Ogunbiyi, I leave that to the care of time. Time will take care of him. Miracles never end, Ola Rotimi might still grow intellectually. For Ola Rotimi's problem is his intellectual pretensions, not some mythical enemies who are supposed to have prevented him from getting his own at the University of Ife.

Rotimi did not bother to reply to this new provocation, but on July 13th Yomi Hussein, a former student at the University of Ife, offered some words "In Defence of Ola Rotimi":

It is very interesting to read all the intellectual pettiness being displayed on the pages of newspapers; only God knows who started it!

As a one-time student of Ife University, this writer had many opportunities to watch both Ola Rotimi and other performers like Wole Soyinka on stage. I cannot but conclude that Ola Rotimi is a first among equals. In his stage productions, his choice of language cuts across the societal spectrum and this makes both an unlettered man from Ife town and the overlettered university professor understand him; unlike those who are not even understood by the social class they profess to be dealing with.

To perceive Ola Rotimi from another angle, here is what commentator Yvonne Neverson of the *Africa Magazine* (May 1978) has to say: "...An African courtyard with a shrine for worshipping the gods...chanting begins off-stage...thus the play *The Gods Are Not to Blame* by Ola Rotimi opens and the set is filled with a colourful spectacle of SERIOUS [emphasis mine] African theatre."

On Ola Rotimi's use of "specific foreign nationals in his plays," what is dramatic arts? If the audience cannot be completely carried away as to believe that they are actually witnessing the events live, those who make do with a normal-sized man where the play requires a midget are only settling with the second best and cannot be regarded as having done justice to what drama should be. We would want Wole [sic] Omotoso to tell his readers whether this is his own idea of nationalism, or another version of the quota system.

As to whether the Yoruba gods are more implacable than those of Greece, a little digression may be necessary here: in this writer's home town in Ogun State, an old man (now dead) consulted the Ifa Oracle in what is normally called "Isepenwo" (i.e., getting a glimpse into what the life of a new born baby will be). It is important here to add that the mother of this new child died during child-bearing. The Ifa priest, without mincing words, told the father that his new child would be an instrument of the father's death. As would be humanly expected, the father asked whether the incident could be averted and some rituals were performed. But as was earlier predicted, the child later poisoned his father in an ambitious move to inherit his property. Unfortunately for the murderer, though, the poisoning effect was slow and the dying man changed his will giving a hopelessly small portion of his property to the desperate son.

As a matter of fact, the authenticity of the will was contested in a court of law and the dispute lasted several years. The case cited above may not be as horrifying as King Oedipus', but one thing stands clear: that little or nothing can be done about prophecy.

Academicians all over the world believe that real intellectual greatness abounds in the ability to research into foreign cultures and bring out what is relevant to the researcher's own culture; if this widely-held opinion is anything to go by, then one begins to wonder why Kole Omotoso is picking bones as to the similarity between Ola Rotimi's *If* and Errol John's *Moon on a Rainbow Shawl*. Art, they say, is not only the ability to create a new horizon, but also improving on what has already been created.

Those who had the opportunity of watching the play *If*, both in Ife, Ibadan and the National Art Theatre in Lagos, confirmed that it is indeed a masterpiece. The Oduduwa Hall of the University of Ife was packed for the four days (Thursday—Sunday) that the play was staged there in 1979. Whether people of Kole Omotoso's creed like it or not, Ola Rotimi is an undisputable King of serious playwrights who deals effectively with both the societal vices and virtues in a way as to leave his audience speechless for hours after leaving the play arena.

The full capacity crowd that watched *If* on that Saturday in 1979 was vividly shown the nakedness and helplessness of our decaying society and people left the hall like mourners dispersing from a burial procession. This magic of mind control, I would say, is possessed by few artists. Any objective analyst of *If* cannot but marvel at Ola Rotimi's accurate prediction of not only the result of the 1979 general election, but the behavioural pattern of the ruling caucus at the centre.

In the light of all these, one begins to wonder whether Kole Omotoso wants us to take him serious about his reference to Ola Rotimi's "intellectual pretension." This phrase is not only misdirected but quite inappropriate when one talks about Ola Rotimi's works. It is a fact all over the ages that no group of people or individual has ever succeeded in suppressing genuine intellectual greatness; a Chief Justice has been moved from office here in Nigeria only to be re-engaged by a higher international law body that knows his worth.

Again, if some of those whom Ola Rotimi used to "summon with whistles" now direct and manage their own productions, as claimed by Kole Omotoso, this would have been a point in favour and not against Ola Rotimi as he would want us to believe. The joy of every lecturer is the number of successful students that passes through his hands. Which, I think, should be the case of Ola Rotimi.

Objective analysts who know Ola Rotimi's worth are happy at his not-too-new job at the University of Port Harcourt. And may he continue to grow in strength.

Future historians of Nigerian theater will no doubt seek to reconstruct what really happened at the Unife Theatre between 1966 and 1985, when Ola Rotimi and Wole Soyinka held sway there and made unique contributions to the development of African performing arts. In assessing the claims and counter-claims made by scores of participants and eyewitnesses, scholars will need to consult what a few interested parties said about those days in the pages of the *Nigerian Tribune* between February and July of 1983, for among the "critical incidentals" and "biased chronicling" recorded there, they may discover clues that will lead them to a more balanced interpretation of contested facts. As every historian knows, any documentary evidence that gives us added insight into the past is too important to be ignored. If truth be asleep, common newsprint could well become the "monkey go wake am."

Works Cited

Abrahams, Peter. "The Long View: African Writers' Part in the Battle against Racial Prejudice." *African World* June 1952: 11-12.

_____. *Return to Goli*. London: Faber, 1953.

Achebe, Chinua. *A Man of the People*. London: Heinemann, 1966.

Adedeji, J.A. "Oral Tradition and the Contemporary Theater in Nigeria." *Research in African Literatures* 2, 2 (1971): 134-149.

Ainslie, Rosalynde. *The Press in Africa: Communications Past and Present*. London: Gollancz, 1966.

Anon. "Getting Through to the South African over the Wall of Words." *Times Literary Supplement* 10 August 1962: 572.

_____. "Black Out." *Times Literary Supplement* 10 May 1963: 341.

_____. "Fabulous Hubert Ogunde." *Spear Magazine* May 1964: 14-17.

_____. "Hubert Ogunde Counts His Blessings!" *Drum* July1965: 31-34.

_____. "Hubert Ogunde—A Musical Celebrity." *The People* February 1970: 8-14, 16-18.

_____. "King of the Stage." *Spear Magazine* February 1972: 4-6.

Anpe, Thomas W. "Hubert Ogunde's Contribution to the Development of Modern Nigerian Theatre." *Nigerian Theatre Journal* [3], 1 (1988): 86-93.

Armah, G.A. "Ut Omnes Unum Sint?"*The Achimotan* (1958): 48-50.

Armah, George. "Editorial." *The Achimotan* (1958): 1.

_____. "School Notes." *The Achimotan* (1958): 2-4.

_____. "Joseph's Fall." *The Achimotan* (1958): 52-56.

_____. "School Notes." *The Achimotan* (1959): 3-5.

_____. "Livingstone House." *The Achimotan* (1959): 28-29.

_____. "One Up or How to Be Somebody." *The Achimotan* (1959): 48-55.

_____. George Sawyerr, A.K. Pianim, Barbara Hyde, and Jane Laing. "Editorial." *The Achimotan* (1959): 1-2.

Bamgbose, Ayo. *The Novels of D.O. Fagunwa*. Benin City: Ethiope Publishing Corp., 1974.

Beier, Ulli. "Fagunwa: A Yoruba Novelist." *Black Orpheus* 17 (1965): 31-56.

_____. "Yoruba Theatre." *Introduction to African Literature*. Ed. Ulli Beier. Evanston, IL: Northwestern University Press, 1967. 243-254.

_____. *The Return of the Gods: The Sacred Art of Suzanne Wenger*. Cambridge: Cambridge University Press, 1975.

Benson, Peter. **Black Orpheus, Transition, and Modern Cultural Awakening in Africa**. Berkeley: University of California Press, 1986.

Bertrand, Etienne. "Le Phénomène 'Ogunde.'" *L'Afrique Littéraire et Artistique* 23 (1972): 72-78.

Bruin, John [pseud. of Dennis Brutus]. *Thoughts Abroad*. Del Valle, TX: Troubadour Press, 1970.

Brutus, Dennis. *Sirens, Knuckles, Boots*. Ibadan: Mbari, 1963.

_____. *Letters to Martha and Other Poems from a South African Prison*. London: Heinemann Educational Books, 1968.

_____. *Poems from Algiers*. Austin: African and Afro-American Research Institute, The University of Texas at Austin, 1970.

_____. "In Memoriam: Arthur Nortje." *Research in African Literatures* 2, 1 (1971): 26-27.

_____. *A Simple Lust*. London: Heinemann Educational Books, 1973.

_____. *China Poems*. Austin: African and Afro-American Studies and Research Center, The University of Texas at Austin, 1975.

_____. *Strains*. Ed. Wayne Kamin and Chip Dameron. Austin: Troubadour Press, 1975.

_____. *Stubborn Hope*. Washington, DC: Three Continents Press, 1978.

Chapman, Michael, ed. *The 'Drum' Decade: Stories from the 1950s*. Pietermaritzburg: University of Natal Press, 1989.

Clark, Ebun. *Hubert Ogunde: The Making of Nigerian Theatre*. Oxford: Oxford University Press, 1979.

Cousins, Norman. "The Man Who Didn't Come to Dinner." *Saturday Review of Literature* 20 April 1957: 38.

Crews, Frederick. *Skeptical Engagements*. New York: Oxford University Press, 1986.

Dodson, Don. "Onitsha Pamphlets: Culture in the Marketplace." Ph.D. dissertation, University of Wisconsin, Madison, 1975.

Ezugu, Michael Amadihe. "The Influence of Theme on Technique in the Novels of Ayi Kwei Armah." Master's thesis, University of Nigeria, Nsukka, 1981.

Fagunwa, D.O. "Writing a Novel." *Teachers' Monthly*, 6, 9 (1960): 12.

Fraser, Robert. *The Novels of Ayi Kwei Armah: A Study in Polemical Fiction*. London: Heinemann Educational Books, 1980.

Graham-White, Anthony. *The Drama of Black Africa*. New York: Samuel French, 1974.

Hachten, William A. *Muffled Drums: The News Media in Africa*. Ames: Iowa State University Press, 1971.

Hall, Barbara, ed. *Tell Me, Josephine*. London: Deutsch, 1964.

Hawkins, Fred. "Too Late to Love." *Drum* October 1955: 46f.

Herdeck, Donald. *African Authors: A Companion to Black African Writing, Volume I: 1300-1973*. Washington, DC: Black Orpheus Press, 1973.

Hogg, Peter, and Ilse Sternberg, eds. *Market Literature from Nigeria: A Checklist*. London: British Library, 1990.

Hopkinson, Tom. "Deaths and Entrances: The Emergence of African Writing." *Twentieth Century* April 1959: 332-342.

_____. *In the Fiery Continent*. London: Gollancz, 1962.

Hussein, Yomi. "In Defence of Ola Rotimi." *Nigerian Tribune* 13 July 1983: 7.

Hutchinson, Alfred. "The Rickshaw's New Year." *Fighting Talk* 11, 10 (December 1957-January 1958): 6-7.

Irele, Abiola. "Tradition and the Yoruba Writer: D.O. Fagunwa, Amos Tutuola and Wole Soyinka." *Odù* n.s. 11 (1975): 75-100.

Jahn, Janheinz, Ulla Schild, and Almut Nordmann. *Who's Who in African Literature: Biographies, Works, Commentaries* Tübingen: Erdmann, 1972.

Jeyifo, 'Biodun. *The Yoruba Popular Travelling Theatre of Nigeria.* Lagos: Department of Culture, Federal Ministry of Social Development, Youth, Sports & Culture, 1984.

July, Robert W. *The Origins of Modern African Thought.* London: Faber, 1968.

Kalitera, Aubrey. *A Taste of Business.* Nairobi: Spear Books, 1976.

_____. *A Prisoner's Letter.* Nairobi: Heinemann Educational Books, 1977.

_____. *Why Father Why.* Blantyre: Power Pen Books, 1982.

_____. *Mother Why Mother.* Blantyre: Power Pen Books, 1983.

_____. *Why Son Why.* Blantyre: Power Pen Books, 1983.

_____. *Daughter Why Daughter.* Blantyre: Power Pen Books, 1983.

_____. *To Ndirande Mountain with Love.* Blantyre: Power Pen Books, 1983.

_____. *She Died in My Bed.* Blantyre: Power Pen Books, 1984.

_____. *Fate.* Blantyre: Power Pen Books, 1984.

_____. *To Felix with Love*. Blantyre: Power Pen Books, 1984.

_____. "Interview with Aubrey Kalitera." *Kulankula: Interviews with Writers from Malawi and Lesotho*. Ed. Bernth Lindfors. African Studies Series, 14. Bayreuth: Bayreuth University, 1989. 3-13.

Ker, David I. "The Short Stories of Ayi Kwei Armah: An Introduction." *Saiwa* 3 (1985): 14-21.

Kitchen, Helen, ed. *The Press in Africa*. Washington, DC: Ruth Sloan Associates, 1956.

La Guma, Alex. "The Machine." *Fighting Talk* 12, 10 (October 1956): 8-9.

_____. "Out of the Darkness." *Africa South* 2, 1 (October-December 1957): 118-122.

_____. *A Walk in the Night*. Ibadan: Mbari, 1962.

_____. *And a Threefold Cord*. Berlin: Seven Seas, 1964.

Lazarus, Neil. *Resistance in Postcolonial African Fiction*. New Haven and London: Yale University Press, 1990.

Lindfors, Bernth. "Amos Tutuola and D.O. Fagunwa." *Journal of Commonwealth Literature* 9 (1970): 57-65.

_____. "John Bruin: South African Enigma in Del Valle, Texas." *Africa Today* 18, 4 (1971): 72-77.

_____, ed. *Palaver: Interviews with Five African Writers in Texas*. Austin: African and Afro-American Research Institute, The University of Texas at Austin, 1972.

_____. "'Somehow Tenderness Survives': Dennis Brutus Talks about His Life and Poetry." *Benin Review* 1 (1974): 44-55.

_____, ed. *South African Voices*. Austin: African and Afro-American Studies Center and the Harry Ransom Center, The University of Texas at Austin, 1975.

Lipenga, Ken. "Interview with Ken Lipenga." *Kulankula: Interviews with Writers from Malawi and Lesotho*. Ed. Bernth Lindfors. African Studies Series, 14. Bayreuth: Bayreuth University, 1989. 14-27.

Maber, Richie. "Way of the Prodigal." *Drum* May 1957: 51f.

Modisane, Bloke. "The Respectable Pickpocket." *Drum* January 1954: 14-15.

_____. "African Writers' Summit." *Transition* 2, 5 (July-August 1962): 5-6.

_____. *Blame Me on History*. London: Thames & Hudson, 1963.

_____. "Short Story Writing in Black South Africa." *American Society of African Culture Newsletter* 5, 8 (March 1963): 2-3.

_____. "The Situation." *Black Orpheus* 12 (1963): 10-16.

Mogale, Arthur. "Crime for Sale." *Drum* January 1953: 33f.

_____. "Hot Diamonds." *Drum* July 1953: 29f.

Mphahlele, Ezekiel. "Blind Alley." *Drum* September 1953: 32-34.

_____. *Down Second Avenue*. London: Faber, 1959.

_____. *The African Image*. London: Faber, 1962.

_____. "An African in America." *Fighting Talk* 16, 1 (February 1962): 10f.

_____. "Mbari—1st Anniversary." *Africa Report* 7, 11 (December 1962): 11-12.

Nkosi, Lewis. "Why 'Bloke' Baled Out." *Contact* 11 July 1959: 6f.

_____. "African Fiction: Part One. South Africa: Protest." *Africa Report* 7, 9 (October 1962): 3-6.

_____. "Conversation with Ezekiel Mphahlele." *Africa Report* 9, 7 (1964): 8-9.

Obiechina, Emmanuel. *An African Popular Literature: A Study of Onitsha Market Pamphlets.* Cambridge: Cambridge University Press, 1973. .

Ogunde, Hubert. "The Life of Hubert Ogunde." *TV Times and Radio News* 25 August 1960: 12-13; 1 September 1960: 4-5.

_____. "My Struggles." *New Era* 2 (March 1973): 19-21.

Olabimtan, Afolabi. "Religion as a Theme in Fagunwa's Novels." *Odù* n.s. 11 (1975): 101-114.

Olubummo, A. "D.O. Fagunwa—A Yoruba Novelist." *Odù* 9 (September 1963): 26-30.

Omotoso, Kole. "Unife Theatre." *Nigerian Tribune* 12 February 1983: 15.

_____. "On Unife Theatre: Ola Rotimi's Last But Not Lasting Word." *Nigerian Tribune* 1 June 1983: 7.

Owomoyela, Oyekan. "Folklore and Yoruba Theater." *Research in African Literatures* 2, 2 (1971): 121-133.

_____. "Obotunde Ijimere, The Phantom of Nigerian Theater." *African Studies Review* 22, 1 (1979): 43-50.

Paton, Alan. "Four Splendid Voices." *Quartet.* Ed. Richard Rive. 11-14.

Rao, K. Damodar. *The Novels of Ayi Kwei Armah.* New Delhi: Prestige Books, 1993.

Ricard, Alain. "The Concert Party as a Genre: The Happy Stars of Lomé." *Research in African Literatures* 5, 2 (1971): 165-179.

Rive, Richard. "Moon Over District Six." *Fighting Talk* 10, 11 (December 1956-January 1957): 7-8.

_____. *African Songs*. Berlin: Seven Seas, 1963.

_____, ed. *Quartet: New Voices from South Africa*. New York: Crown, 1963.

_____. "Moçambique Writing." *New African* 2, 6 (July 1963): 121-122.

_____. *Emergency*. London: Faber, 1964.

Rotimi, Ola. "Unife Theatre: Ola Rotimi Speaks." *Nigerian Tribune* 19 March 1983: 7; 23 March 1983: 7; 26 March 1983: 7.

_____. "Unife Theatre: My Last Word." *Nigerian Tribune* 27 April 1983: 7.

Sampson, Anthony. *Drum: A Venture into the New Africa*. London: Collins, 1956.

Schild, Ulla. "Janheinz Jahn, 1918-1973." *Research in African Literatures* 5 (1974): 194-195.

_____. "A Bibliography of the Works of Janheinz Jahn." *Research in African Literatures* 5 (1974): 196-205.

Sefora, Rita. "I Was in a Dream-land." *Drum* January 1953: 23f.

Segal, Ronald. *Into Exile*. London: Jonathan Cape, 1963.

Soyinka, Wole. "Unife Theatre: A Correction." *Nigerian Tribune* 16 April 1983: 7.

_____. "Of Exits and Entrances: The Late Hubert Ogunde." *Sunday Times* 15 April 1990: 9.

Themba, Can. "Passionate Stranger." *Drum* March 1953: 24-25.

_____. "Mob Passion." *Drum* April 1953: 22f.

Wilkov, A. *Some English Writings by Non-Europeans in South Africa.* Johannesburg: University of the Witwatersrand, 1962.

Wright, Derek. "The Early Writings of Ayi Kwei Armah." *Research in African Literatures* 16 (1985): 487-513.

_____. *Ayi Kwei Armah's Africa: The Sources of His Fiction.* London: Hans Zell, 1989.

_____. "Ayi Kwei Armah and the Significance of His Novels and Stories." *International Fiction Review* 17 (1990): 29-40.

INDEX

Index

Abakaliki, Nigeria, 124
Abbia, 51
Abby, 128
Abeokuta, Nigeria, 148, 152
Abiakam, J., 49 Wise Sayings, 72 Idioms, 44 Questions and Answers and Some Speeches of World Leaders Past and Present, 111
Abiku, 45
Abrahams, Peter, 16-17, 26, 38, 185
Achebe, Chinua, 30, 32, 38, 43-44, 54, 73-74, 100, 107, 115, 185; A Man of the People, 32, 115; "The Voter," 32
Achimota School, 53-69
Achimotan, The, 55-68
Addition, 111-13
Ade, Sunny, 172
Adebona, Dr., 168
Adedeji, Joel, 145, 173, 185
Adejobi Theatre Group, 169
Adelugba, Dapo, 173
Adenuga, G.A., 148
Aesop, Fables, 141
Afa, 49
Afolabi, Jacob, 31
"Africa and God" (Ogunde), 150, 154

Africa Magazine, 181
Africa South, 7-8, 13
Africa South in Exile, 7
Africa Today, 98
African-Americans, 5, 23, 25, 28, 32-33, 38, 40
African and Afro-American Research Institute, University of Texas at Austin, 92-94
African and Afro-American Studies Program, University of Texas at Austin, 99
African Bethel School, Ijebu Ode, Nigeria, 147
African Drum, 4-5
African Guardian, The, 44
African language literature, 3
African Literature Association, 99-101
African Literature Today, 47
African Personality, 30
African Songs (Rive), 18
African Studies Association, 99
African Theatre Review, 49, 51
African Writers Series, 91, 99
Afrikaans, 3, 95
Afro-Cuban literature, 25
Ahmadu Bello University, 51

Aidoo, [Christina] Ama Ata, 28, 100
Ainslie, Rosalynde, 120, 185
Ajaiyi and His Inherited Poverty (Tutuola), 32
"Ajaiyi and the Witchdoctor" (Tutuola), 32
Ajayi, Gboyega, 169
Akan, 26, 35-37
Akanji, Adebisi, 31
Akanji, Sangodare, 32
Akinbola, Segun, 169
Akpabot, Sam, 165-66; *Jaja of Opobo*, 166
Aku, Aper, 162
Akure, Nigeria, 120
Aladoro Church, Lagos, 150
Alawada theatre, 174
Algeria, 30
Algiers, 92-93, 98
al-Hakim, Tawfiq, 180
Allen, Samuel W., 25-26
Amali, Samson, 35
Amao, Ayan, 171-72, 178
Amharic, 30
Amin, Idi, 47
Amoo, Anyantunji, 169, 175-76
And a Threefold Cord (La Guma), 18
Angola, 29-30
Anjorin, Mrs. Yinka, 169
Anpe, Thomas W., 145, 185
Antigua, 40
Anyidoho, Kofi, 40
Arabian Nights, The, 141

Arabic, 34, 168, 181
Arab-Muslim, 180
Aragbabalu, Omidiji, 32
Architecture, 37
Arigbede, Seinde, 169
Aristotle, 170
Armah, Ayi Kwei, 53-69, 73-74, 186; *The Beautyful Ones Are Not Yet Born*, 53; "Contact," 53, 63; "Joseph's Fall," 59-63; "Livingstone House," 66; "One Up or How to Be Somebody," 66-67; "School Notes," 65-66; "Ut Omnes Unum Sint?" 58-59; *Why Are We So Blest?* 53, 63
Armstrong, Louis "Satchmo," 5
Aro, 43
Art, 23, 25, 27, 29, 31, 34-35, 37, 39
Artist's Pot, The, 47
Arubidi, Ife, Nigeria, 161
Asiru, 31
Association of Nigerian Authors, 162
Atlantic Monthly, 53
Attarrah, Christina, 28
Augean stable, 109
Austin, Texas, 92-110, 122
Awoonor, Kofi, 28, 100
Awoonor-Williams, George, 28
Ayansola, 176

"Ayomo" (Ogunde), 155

Babalawo, 153
Babalola, Adeboye, 23
Badejo, Peter, 169
Balzac, Honoré de, 56
Bambara, 27
Bamgbose, Ayo, 137, 141, 186
Banham, Martin, 38
Bantu, 4
Baptist Church, Ijebu-Ife, 146
Baptist School, Ife, 147, 154
Baptist Seminary,
    Ogbomosho, 154
Baraza, 50
Barrett, Lindsay, 34
Bart-Williams, Gaston, 28
Basutos, 5
Bayeke, 26
Beacon, 43
*Beautyful Ones Are Not Yet
    Born, The* (Armah), 53
Beier, Georgina, 31
Beier, Ulli, 23-24, 27, 31-33,
    40-41, 137, 145, 186; *The
    Imprisonment of Obatala*,
    31; *Woyengi*, 31
Belfast, 98
Belgian Congo, 27
Bemba, Sylvain, 30
Benin City, Nigeria, 121
Benin Review, The, 38, 99
Benson, Peter, 41, 52, 186
Bently, Miss, 57
Berlin, 18
Berriman, Mr., 57

Bertrand, Etienne, 146, 186
Beti, Mongo, 30, 73
*Beware of Harlots and Many
    Friends: The World is Hard*,
    108
Bhêly-Quénum, Olympe, 30
Biafra, 33, 35
Bible, 118, 127, 150
Biko Inquest, The, 179
"Black Forest, The"
    (Ogunde), 150
Black Orpheus, 23-41, 44, 46
Black Power (Wright), 23
Black Studies, 92
Blame Me on History
    (Modisane), 18
Blantyre, Malawi, 75, 77, 85
Bognini, Joseph Miezan, 29
Bordeaux, France, 94
Bosman, H.C., 94
Boston University, 170-71
Brathwaite, Edward,
    "Harmattan Poems," 38;
    Rights of Passage, 35
Brazil, 29-30
Brecht, Bertolt, 173
Bristol, England, 98
British: humor, 139; press,
    120, 155; West Africa, 118
Bruin, Fanie du Mealie, 97
Bruin, John, 97-98, 187;
    Thoughts Abroad, 97-99
Brutus, Dennis, 18, 20, 28, 38,
    91-103, 187; *China Poems*,
    101; *Letters to Martha and
    Other Poems from a South*

African Prison, 91, 93, 98;
Poems from Algiers, 93, 98,
101; *A Simple Lust*, 99;
Sirens, Knuckles, Boots, 18,
91, 93, 98; *Strains*, 102;
Stubborn Hope, 102;
Thoughts Abroad, 97-99
Buddy Bradley School of
Dancing, 151
Bunyan, John, 57; *The
Pilgrim's Progress*, 139, 141
Buraimoh, Tunji, 169

Cairo, 98
*Calabar Studies in Modern
Languages*, 48-49
Caldwell, Erskine, 19
Caliban, 36
California, 171
Cambridge School
Certificate, 54, 66
Cameroon, 157
*Cameroon Studies in English
and French*, 49
Cameroons, 29-30
Campbell, Roy, 94
Canadian Expo, 155
Cape Argus, The, 9
Cape Coast, Ghana, 53
Cape Times, 9
Cape Town, 8, 14, 20
Carew, Jan, 30
Cary, Joyce, 26
Celebration, 47
Censorship, 8, 19-20, 27, 96,
98

Central Africa, 29
Centre for Cultural Studies,
University of Lagos, 172
Césaire, Aimé, 25, 28
Chaka, 166
Chancellor College, 49-51, 75
Chandra, A., 31
Chapbooks, 30, 107-115
Chapman, Michael, 21, 187
Chase, James Hadley, 9, 88
Chaucer, Geoffrey, 63, 141;
"Troilus and Criseyde,"
63
Chestnut Theatre, 167
Cheyney, Peter, 9
Cheyney-Coker, Syl, 40
Chicago, 99
Chimombo, Steve, 50
China, People's Republic of,
101
China Poems (Brutus), 101
Chinatown, 170
Ch'indaba, 44
Ching-Po, Ko, 102
Chipasula, Frank, 50
Christian Missionary Society,
118
Christianity, 143
Civil war, Nigeria, 44, 158
Clark, Ebun, 39, 145, 187
Clark, John Pepper, 27, 30-31,
33-34, 36, 38-39, 43-44;
"The Imprisonment of
Obatala," 31; "The
Legacy of Caliban," 36;
Ozidi, 36;

Classic, The, 8, 21
Comfymanship, 67
Conateh, Swaebou, 40
Concert party, 145, 152-53
Congo, 28, 30, 37, 120
Congress for Cultural
    Freedom, 24
*Constitution of the Communist
    Party of China, The*, 19
"Contact" (Armah), 53, 63
"Corpse in the Lift," 6
Cortez, Jayne, 38
Couchoro, Felix, 40
Cousins, Norman, 4, 187
Crews, Frederick, 45-46, 187
Criseyde, 63
Crowder, Michael, 168
Cry, the Beloved Country
    (Paton), 5
Cuba, 34
Cugoano, Ottobah, 38
Curse, The (Omotoso), 160,
    166, 180
Customs Act (1955), 19

Dahomey, 27, 30, 131
Daily Mirror, 119
Daily Sketch, 120-21
Daily Times, 119, 121, 132, 146
Damas, Leon, 31
Dameron, Chip, 102
Dandymanship, 66
Dark Child, The (Laye), 23
Darwulla, K.N., 29
Datsun, 172

Daughter Why Daughter
    (Kalitera), 86-87
Dawes, Carroll, 176
de Mille, Agnes, 170
Death and the King's Horseman
    (Soyinka), 179
Defoe, Daniel, *Robinson
    Crusoe*, 141
Del Valle, Texas, 97
Deletion, 111-12
Denga, 50
Detention Act, 20
Dickens, Charles, 9
Diete-Spiff, Commander, 131
Diop, Birago, 73
Diop, David, 25, 73
Dipoko, Mbella Sonne, 29
Disaster in the Realms of Love,
    108
District Six, Cape Town, 14-
    15
Doctor Faustus (Marlowe),
    141
Dodson, Don, 115, 188
Dotchmanship, 67
Dream on Monkey Mountain
    (Walcott), 176
*Dr. Nkrumah in the Struggle
    for Freedom*, 108
Drum, 4-13, 15, 17-18, 20-21,
    74
*Drum: A Venture into the New
    Africa* (Sampson), 21
Drums, 35-37
Dubrovnik, 98

Dugbe Market, Ibadan, Nigeria, 149
Dumile, Feni, 97
Dunaway, Faye, 170-71

Eagle, The, 43
East Africa, 28-29, 37, 120
East Central State, Nigeria, 146
Echeruo, Michael, 27
Egba, 118
Egudu, Romanus, 29, 100
Egypt, 30, 180
Eiyeire (Ogunde), 155
Ekiye, Comish, *The Family*, 160, 166
Ekwensi, Cyprian, 26, 73, 75, 107
Ekwueme, Vice-President, 162
Ellington, Duke, 5
Emergency (Rive), 18
England, 32, 91, 95, 151, 153, 155
English language, 3, 27, 34, 109, 113
Enugu, Nigeria, 121, 149
Esuene, K.J., 131
Ethiopia, 31
Euba, Akin, 34, 38, 165-66
Europe, 37, 73, 94, 118, 140, 151, 155, 158
Eurydice, 24
Eva Peron, 170
Ewe, 26
Exile, 16-18

Eze, Charles N., *Learn to Speak 360 Interesting Proverbs and Know Your True Brother*, 111
Ezugu, Michael Amadihe, 69, 188

Fables (Aesop), 141
Fabunmi, Adebisi, 31
Faerie Queene, The (Spenser), 139, 141
Fagunwa, Daniel Olorunfemi, 30, 137-43, 188; *The Forest of a Thousand Daemons*, 141; "Writing a Novel," 137-40
Faji, Lagos, 154
Falashas, 31
Family, The (Ekiye), 160, 166
Farfield Foundation, 8
Fighting Talk, 7, 14, 20
Fleming, Ian, 88
Florence in the River of Temptation, 108
Folarin, Margaret, 168
Forest of a Thousand Daemons (Fagunwa), 141
Fourah Bay Studies in Language and Literature, 48
France, 155, 170
Francis, Reynold S., 40
Frankfurt, 98
Fraser, Robert, 53, 188
Frasers, 57

French, 168; Congo, 128;
West Africans, 25-28, 33
Fresh Buds, 47
Friendship International
Table Tennis Tournament,
101

Gable, Clark, 12
Gambia, The, 28, 40, 118
Ganga, 49
"Garden of Eden, The"
(Ogunde), 150, 154-55
Gardner, Erle Stanley, 88
Garvey, Marcus, 37
Gassner, John, 171
Gates, Henry Louis, Jr., 44
Germany, 18, 29, 32, 34, 167,
170
Ghana, 26, 28, 34-35, 37, 40,
53-69, 74, 151-53, 157-58,
170; Dance Ensemble, 35
Gibbs, James, 69
Gikuyu, 74
Glover Memorial Hall,
Lagos, 150
Gods Are Not to Blame, The
(Rotimi), 166, 180-81
Goethe, Johann Wolfgang
von, 167
Gold Coast, 56, 118
Golden City Post, 6, 9
Gordimer, Nadine, 94-95, 98
Government Gazette, 19
Graham-White, Anthony,
146, 188
Greece, 182

Greek, 180; mythology, 141
Grenoble, 98
Groton School, 53-54
Group Areas Act, 15
Guadeloupe, 34
Guedes, Pedro, 31
Guiana, 30, 34, 40
Guinea, 26-27, 29-30, 33
Gwala, T.H., 7
Gwani, 49

Hachten, William A., 118,
188
Hades, 24
Hadramaut, 180
Hall, Barbara, 133, 188
Hamlet (Shakespeare), 172
"Harmattan Poems"
(Brathwaite), 38
Harper, Peggy, 165-66
Harper's Magazine, 53
Harvard University, 8, 53
Hausa, 31
Hawkins, Fred, 13, 188
Hayden, Robert, 39
Heinemann Educational
Books Ltd., 76, 91, 99
Hekima, 49
Hemingway, Ernest, 19
"Herbert Macaulay"
(Ogunde), 151
Herdeck, Donald, 145, 188
Higo, Aig, 34
Hogg, Peter, 115, 188
Holmes, Sherlock, 157
Hopalong Cassidy, 19

Hopkinson, Tom, 16, 21, 188;
In the Fiery Continent, 21
Horn, The, 43, 47
Hotop, G.M., 23
*How a Passenger Collector
Posed and Got a Lady
Teacher in Love*, 108
*How Lumumba Suffered in Life
and Died in Katanga*, 108
*How to Live Bachelor's Life and
Girl's Life without Much
Mistakes*, 108
*How to Marry a Good Girl and
Live in Peace with Her*, 108
*How to Write Good English and
Compositions*, 108
*How to Write Love Letters,
Toasts and Business Letters*,
108
Hughes, Langston, 25, 28
"Human Parasites"
(Ogunde), 150
Humanities Research Center
(HRC), University of
Texas at Austin, 94-96, 98
Hussein, Yomi, 181, 188
Hutchinson, Alfred, 7, 15, 17,
189

"I Broke Their Hearts," 10
"I Was in a Dream-land," 10
*Ibadan Journal of Humanistic
Studies*, 49
Ibadan, Nigeria, 29, 35, 121-
22, 131, 148, 152, 167, 182
Ibadan University, 29, 43, 47

Idah, I., 31
Idoma, 35
Idoto, 47
If (Rotimi), 181-83
Ifa, 35; oracle, 182
Ife Festival of the Arts, 159
*Ife Monographs on Literature
and Criticism*, 49
Ife, Nigeria, 154, 157-84
*Ife Studies in African Literature
and the Arts*, 49
Ife Writing, 47
Igbo: chapbooks, 74;
economic activity, 107;
oral tradition, 114;
people, 35; poetry, 31;
poets, 37; writers, 33, 115
Ijala, 23
Ijala, 47
Ijaw: folktale, 31; journal, 43;
myths, 26; saga, 35
Ijebu-Ife, Nigeria, 146
Ijebu Ode, Nigeria, 146-47,
154
Ijebu Province, Nigeria, 148
Ijimere, Obotunde, 31
Impressionmanship, 66-67
Imprisonment of Obatala, The
(Beier), 31
"Imprisonment of Obatala,
The" (Clark), 31
In the Fiery Continent
(Hopkinson), 21
India, 29, 32, 34, 120
Indonesia, 32
Innes, Hammond, 88

Institute of African Studies, University of Ife, 159, 164
International Comparative Literature Association, 94
Iran, 32
Irele, Abiola, 24, 33-34, 38, 99, 137, 189
Isepenwo, 182
"Israel and Egypt" (Ogunde), 150
Italy, 155
Ivory Coast, 27, 29, 151
Iwe Irohin fun awon ara Egba Yorubas, 118

Jahn, Janheinz, 23-24, 41, 145, 189
Jaja of Opobo (Akpabot), 166
Jamaica, 29-30, 34
James, E.A., 26
Jesus Christ, 131
Jeyifo, Biodun, 100, 145, 189
Johannesburg, 4, 9, 12, 20
John, Errol, *Moon on a Rainbow Shawl*, 181-82
Jones, Horatio Edward Babatunde, 28
Jones, LeRoi, 29
Jos, Nigeria, 151-52, 155
"Joseph's Fall" (Armah), 59-63
Journal of the Performing Arts, 49
"Journey to Heaven" (Ogunde), 150
July, Robert W., 119, 189

Kachingwe, Aubrey, 76
Kaduna, Nigeria, 121, 152
Kalitera, Aubrey, 73-90, 189; *Daughter Why Daughter*, 86-87; *Mother Why Mother*, 87, 89; *A Prisoner's Letter*, 76, 79; *She Died in My Bed*, 77, 87; *A Taste of Business*, 76, 79, 81-83, 87-88; *To Felix with Love*, 86; *To Ndirande Mountain with Love*, 79, 86-87; *Why Father Why*, 79, 83-85, 87-89; *Why Son Why*, 86, 89
Kalulu, 50
Kamin, Wayne, 100, 102
Kano, Nigeria, 152
Kathir, Ali Ahmad, 180
Keene, Laura, 167
Kennedy, Edward, 131
Kennedy, Robert, 131
Kent, Duchess of, 56-57
Kenya, 28, 31, 49, 76
Ker, David, 190
Kgositsile, Keorapetse, 100
Kiabàrà, 49
Kibi, Ghana, 57
King, Bruce, 34
"King of Crime," 6
"King Solomon" (Ogunde), 150, 154-55
Kironde, Erisa, 39
Kiswahili. See Swahili.
Kitchen, Helen, 190
Kofi, Vincent Akweti, 29

Konadu, S.A., *A Woman in Her Prime*, 35
Kono, 27
Kosygin, Alexei, 131
Krea, Henri, 30
Krige, Uys, 95
Kuka, 51
Kunene, Dan, 100
Kunene, Mazisi, 92, 100
Kurunmi (Rotimi), 164, 166, 169, 180

Ladipo, Duro, 169
Lagos, Nigeria, 39, 41, 119, 121, 132, 145-46, 149-50, 152-54, 169, 182
Lagos Review of English Studies, 49
Lagos Weekend, 121
La Guma, Alex, 7, 13-16, 18, 20, 26, 28, 92, 190; *And a Threefold Cord*, 18; "Out of the Darkness," 13; *A Walk in the Night*, 18
"Lament of the Lavender Mist" (Okigbo), 31
Lashley, Cliff, 29-30
Latin, 30; America, 32
Lawrence, D.H., 29
Laye, Camara, 23, 26, 30, 38, 40, 73; *The Dark Child*, 23
Lazarus, Neil, 53, 190
Learn to Speak 360 Interesting Proverbs and Know Your True Brother (Eze), 111

"Legacy of Caliban, The" (Clark), 36
Lenin, Nikolai, 19
Letters to Martha and Other Poems from a South African Prison (Brutus), 91, 93, 98
Library of Congress, 98
"Life of Hubert Ogunde, The" (Ogunde), 146-53
Life Story and Death of John Kennedy, The, 108
Life Turns Man Up and Down; Money and Girls Turn Man Up and Down, 109
Lindfors, Bernth, 190-91
Lipenga, Ken, 50, 191
Literary criticism, 26-28, 30, 36
Literature Students Association, Nairobi, 47
"Livingstone House" (Armah), 66
Lomé, 153
London, 7, 18, 76, 91-92, 94, 96, 98-99, 107, 119, 151
Longmans, 24
Los Angeles, 91
Luo, 29
Lyndersay, Dexter, 180

Mabel the Sweet Honey that Poured Away, 108
Maber, Richie, 13, 191
Macaulay, Herbert, 151
McCartney, Barney, 98, 100
McGovern, George, 131

McKay, Claude, 30
Madagascar, 28
Maddy, Pat, 173
Maillu, David, 75
Maimane, Arthur, 28
Makerere Beat, 47
Makerere University College,
     43-44, 47
Malangatana, Valente
     Goenha, 29
Malawi, 29, 49-51, 73-90, 157
Malawi News, 79
Mali, 27
Malozi, 29
Mammy Water, 43
Man of the People, A (Achebe),
     32, 115
Mapanje, Jack, 50
Marang, 49
Marlowe, Christopher, *Doctor
     Faustus*, 141
Martinique, 25
Marx, Karl, 19
Mason, Mason Jordan, 25
Matshikiza, Todd, 17
Matthews, James, 9, 12
Mayakiri, Tijani, 169
Mazrui, Ali, 37, 100
Mbabane, Swaziland, 98
Mbari Centre, 18, 27, 91
Melville J. Herskovits
     Africana Library, 96
Mercedes Benz, 175
Merchant of Venice
     (Shakespeare), 113
Metalious, Grace, 19

Mexico City, 91
Milton, John, 141
Ministry of Education,
     Nigeria, 24, 137, 139
Mirror, The, 51
*Miss Cordelia in the Romance
     of Destiny*, 108
Mnthali, Felix, 50
"Mob Passion" (Themba), 12-
     13
Modisane, Bloke, 4, 12, 16-18,
     28, 191; *Blame Me on
     History*, 18; "The
     Situation," 18
Mogale, Arthur, 11, 191
*Money Hard to Get but Easy to
     Spend*, 108
Moody, H.L., 168
Moon on a Rainbow Shawl
     (John), 181-82
"Moon Over District Six"
     (Rive), 14-15
Moore, Gerald, 23, 37
Moscow Art Theatre, 167
Mosher, Marlene, 40
Mother Why Mother
     (Kalitera), 87, 89
Mould, 49, 51
Mozambique, 29, 31
Mphahlele, Ezekiel [Es'kia],
     3-5, 9-10, 12, 16-18, 24-26,
     37, 73-74, 94, 100, 191
"Mr. Devil's Money"
     (Ogunde), 151
Mtshali, Oswald, 100; *Sounds
     of a Cowhide Drum*, 21

Munich, 121
Muse, The (Nsukka), 49
Muse, The (Zomba), 49-50
Mwangaza wa Fasihi, 47
"My Husband Was a Flirt,"
    10
*My Seven Daughters are after
    Young Boys*, 108
"My Struggles" (Ogunde),
    153-55
Myths, 29, 31
Mzalendo, 47

Nagenda, John, 44
Nagler, Alois, 171
Nairobi, Kenya, 76, 79
Nakasa, Nat, 8
Nandi, Fiji, 98
National Art Theatre, 182
National Concord, 174
National Theatre, Nigeria,
    145
National Troupe, Nigeria, 145
Nazareth, Peter, 44, 100
Ndu, Pol N., 29, 100
"Nebukanezzer's Reign"
    (Ogunde), 150
Neo-Tarzanism, 177-78
Neto, Agostinho, 29-30
Neverson, Yvonne, 181
New African, The, 7-8, 53
New Age, 7
New Delhi, 98
New Horizons, 49, 51
New Nigerian, 121
New York City, 98, 171

Newspapers, 117-33, 157-84
Newsweek, 121
Ngam, 49, 51
Ngoma, 49
Ngugi wa Thiong'o [James],
    43-44, 47, 54, 73-74
Nieman Fellowship, 8
Niger River, 107
Nigeria, 23, 25-35, 37-40, 44,
    48-49, 51, 74-75, 91, 99,
    107-84
*Nigerian Journal of the
    Humanities*, 49
Nigerian Theatre Journal, 49
Nigerian Tide, 121
Nigerian Tribune, 121, 158-84
Nixon, Richard, 57, 131
*NJALA: New Approaches to
    Language Arts*, 49
Njoku, N.U., *Teach Your-self
    Proverbs, Idioms, Wise
    Sayings, Laws, Rights of a
    Citizen, English
    Applications and Many
    Other Things for Schools
    and Colleges*, 111
Nkà, 49
Nketia, J.H. Kwabena, 35-37
Nkosi, Lewis, 4, 16-17, 191
*No Money, Much Expenses,
    Enemies and Bad Friends
    Kill a Man*, 108
Nordmann, Almut, 189
North America, 91
Northwestern University, 96,
    99

Nortje, Arthur, 28, 93, 96
Nsukka, Nigeria, 29
Nsukka Studies in African Literature, 49
Nsukkascope, 44
NTV-Lagos, 169
Nwankwo, Nkem, 28
Nwapa, Flora, 39
Nwoko, Demas, 29, 31, 34-35
Nyang, Sulayman S., 39

*O*balúayé (Ogunyemi), 166
Obeya, 175
Obiechina, Emmanuel, 100, 115, 192
Obilade, Tony, 169
Observer, 121
Odi, 50
Oduduwa Hall, 160-61, 164-65, 172, 176
Odyssey, The, 141
Oedipus, 180, 182
Oedipus Rex (Sophocles), 180
Ofirima, 47
Ogot, Grace, 28
Ogun State, Nigeria, 182
Ogunba, Oyin, 35, 37, 173
Ogunbiyi, Yemi, 173-74, 181
Ogunde, Clementina, 152-53
Ogunde, Eunice Owotusam, 154
Ogunde, Hubert, 39, 145-55, 167, 173-74, 192; "Africa and God," 150, 154; "Ayomo," 155; "The Black Forest," 150; *Eiyeire*, 155; "The Garden of Eden," 150, 154-55; "Herbert Macaulay," 151; "Human Parasites," 150; "Israel and Egypt," 150; "Journey to Heaven," 150; "King Solomon," 150, 154-55; "The Life of Hubert Ogunde," 146-53; "Mr. Devil's Money," 151; "My Struggles," 153-55; "Nebukanezzer's Reign," 150; *Onijonimi*, 155; *Orilonishe*, 155; "Strike and Hunger," 150-52, 154-55; "The Tiger's Empire," 151; "Towards Liberty," 151; *Yeyemi*, 155; "Yoruba Ronu," 155; "Yours Forever," 151
Ogunde, Jeremiah Dehinbo, 146, 154
Ogundele, Rufus, 31
Ogunyemi, Wale, *Obalúayé*, 166
Okafor, Clem. Abiaziem, 29
Okara, Gabriel, 23, 25, 27-28, 31-32, 38, 40; *The Voice*, 32
Oke Ona United School, Abeokuta, Nigeria, 148
Okeowo, Yinka, 169
Okigbo, Christopher, 27, 31, 34-37, 47; "Lament of the Lavender Mist," 31; "Path of Thunder," 35
Okike, 44-45

Okot p'Bitek, 35, 37; *Song of Lawino*, 35
Okyeame, 53
Olabimtan, Afolabi, 137, 192
Olubummo, A., 137, 192
Oluwasanmi, Hezekiah, 165
Olympics, 91, 121
Omabe, 47
Omogbai, Colette, 31
Omotoso, Kole, 45, 159-84; *The Curse*, 160, 166, 180
One Hundred Popular Facts about "Sex and Facts," 108
"One Up or How to Be Somebody" (Armah), 66-67
Onigbinde, Ade, 169
Onijonimi (Ogunde), 155
Onitsha market chapbooks, 30, 46, 74, 107-115
Onitsha, Nigeria, 107
Onobrakpeya, Bruce, 35
Onyejeli, Bona, 29
Oral literature, 23, 26-27, 29-30, 33, 35, 40, 51
Ori Olokun Players, 169
Orilonishe (Ogunde), 155
Oron, Nigeria, 124
Orpheus, 24
Ososa, Nigeria, 146-47, 152, 154
Oti, Sonny, 173
Our Africa, 6
"Out of the Darkness" (La Guma), 13
Outlook, 50

Ovonramwen Nogbaisi (Rotimi), 169
Owiti, Hezbon, 31
Owolabi, Leke, 168
Owomoyela, Oyekan, 41, 145, 192
Oyelami, Muraina, 31, 169
Oyono, Ferdinand, 38, 73
Ozidi (Clark), 36

Palaver: Interviews with Five African Writers in Texas, 94
Palm-Wine Drinkard, The (Tutuola), 23
Pan-African Cultural Festival, 92-93
Pandarus, 63
Papua New Guinea, 32
Paris, 23, 30, 98, 151
Parker, Carolyn, 99
"Passionate Intruder," 6
"Passionate Stranger" (Themba), 11
"Path of Thunder" (Okigbo), 35
Paton, Alan, 3, 5, 18, 192; *Cry, the Beloved Country*, 5
Peace Corps, 34
Penpoint, 44, 47
Persian, 34
Peters, Lenrie, 28
Peugeot, 172
Phantasia novel, 138-43
Piccadilly Circus, London, 151

Pieterse, Cosmo, 92, 100
Pilgrim's Progress, The
    (Bunyan), 139, 141
Pit Theatre, University of Ife,
    161
Plato, 175
Playboy, 19
Pluto, 24
Poems from Algiers (Brutus),
    93, 98, 101
Police Training College,
    Enugu, Nigeria, 149
Pope, 127
Port Elizabeth, South Africa,
    93
Port Harcourt, Nigeria, 121,
    124, 159, 170
Povey, John, 92
Power Pen Books, 75, 79, 85,
    89
Présence Africaine, 24
Présence Africaine, 53
Prisoner's Letter, A (Kalitera),
    76, 79
Progressive Party, 43
Prospero, 36
Proverbs, 107-115
Publications and
    Entertainments Act
    (1963), 20
Pula, 49

Quartet, 18
Queen, Ellery, 19

Rabéarivelo, Jean-Joseph, 28

Ranaivo, Flavien, 28
Ransom, Harry, 94-96, 102
Rao, K. Damodar, 53, 192
Rearrangement, 111, 113
Reid, George, 168
Renaissance, 121
Requiem for a Futurologist
    (Soyinka), 179
Research in African Literatures,
    92-93
Ricard, Alain, 145, 193
Rights of Passage (Brathwaite),
    35
Rive, Richard, 7, 12, 14-16,
    18-19, 193; *African Songs*,
    18; *Emergency*, 18; "Moon
    Over District Six," 14-15
Rivers State, Nigeria, 131
Robben Island, 20
Robin Hood, 30
Robinson Crusoe (Defoe), 141
Robinson, Femi, 168
Rock'n'Roll Manship, 67
Rome, 98
Rose Only Loved My Money,
    108
Rotimi, Ola, 157-84, 193; *The
    Gods Are Not to Blame*,
    166, 180-81; *If*, 181-83;
    Kurunmi, 164, 166, 169,
    180; *Ovonramwen
    Nogbaisi*, 169
Rubadiri, David, 29
"Runaway Bride," 6
Runyon, Damon, 11

St. John's C.M.S. School, Ososa, Nigeria, 147, 154
St. Louis, Missouri, 120
Saint Peters School, Faji, Lagos, 154
Saiwa, 49, 51
Sala, Baba, 167
Salahi, Ibrahim, 29
Salami, Sabit Adeyboyega, 40
Salinger, J.D., 19
Salkey, Andrew, 26
Sampson, Anthony, *Drum: A Venture into the New Africa*, 21, 193
Sanchez, Sonia, 39
Sancho, Ignatius, 38
Saro-Wiwa, Ken, 34
Sartre, Jean-Paul, 24
Satchmo, 5
Saturday Night Disappointment, 108
Schild, Ulla, 189, 193
"School Notes" (Armah), 65-66
Schreiner, Olive, 94
Schultz, Diane, 171
Security Police, South African, 8
Sefora, Rita, 10, 193
Segal, Ronald, 7, 193
Sekondi, Ghana, 53
Senghor, Léopold Sédar, 23-25, 28, 40, 73
Sepamla, Sipho, 21
Seroke, Jaki, 21

Serote, Mongane Wally, 100
Seven Seven, Twins, 31
Seyaseya, Chinjara Hopewell, 40
Shakespeare, William, 9, 141; *Hamlet*, 172; *Merchant of Venice*, 113; *The Tempest*, 36
She Died in My Bed (Kalitera), 77, 87
Sherwood, Mr., 57
Shibrain, 31
Sholu sisters, 169
Sierra Leone, 28, 40, 118
Simon, Barney, 8
Simple Lust, A (Brutus), 99
Sirens, Knuckles, Boots (Brutus), 18, 91, 93, 98
"Situation, The" (Modisane), 18
Small Enterprise Development Organization of Malawi (SEDOM), 78
Sofola, Zulu, 173
Sofoluwe, Akin, 169
Sokoti, 47
Song of Lawino (Okot), 35
Sophocles, *Oedipus Rex*, 180
Sounds of a Cowhide Drum (Mtshali), 21
South Africa, 3-21, 25-28, 30, 37, 74, 91, 93-98, 100
South African Bantu languages, 74

South African Non-Racial Olympic Committee (SANROC), 91
South African Outlook, 98
South African Table Tennis Board, 101
South African Voices, 101
South-Eastern State, Nigeria, 131
Southern Bantu literature, 30
Sowande, Bode, 169
Soyinka, Wole, 24-25, 27, 30, 38, 43-44, 54, 73-74, 145, 157-84, 193; *Death and the King's Horseman*, 179; *Requiem for a Futurologist*, 179
Spellman, A.B., 29
Spenser, Edmund, *The Faerie Queene*, 139, 141
Spillane, Mickey, 19
Stalin, Joseph, 19
Stanislavsky, Constantin, 167, 170, 173
Statements of Hitler before the World War, The, 108
Steinhart, Ed, 99
Sternberg, Ilse, 115, 188
Stockholm, 98
Strains (Brutus), 102
Streak, 117, 133
"Strike and Hunger" (Ogunde), 150-52, 154-55
Stubborn Hope (Brutus), 102
Student's Eye, The, 47
Stuffmanship, 66

Substitution, 111-13
Sudan, 29, 31
Sunday Observer, 121, 128
Sunday Post, 121
Sunday Punch, 121
Sunday Sketch, 121, 132
Sunday Times, 121
Suppression of Communism Act (1950), 19-20
Swahili, 29, 34, 74
Sweden, 32, 34
Sweet Mag, 76-77, 79
Sydney, 98
Syllabus, 51

Table Mountain, 14
Tanzania, 157
Taste of Business, A (Kalitera), 76, 79, 81-83, 87-88
Teach Your-self Proverbs, Idioms, Wise Sayings, Laws, Rights of a Citizen, English Applications and Many Other Things for Schools and Colleges (Njoku), 111
Teachers' Monthly, 137
Tehran, 98
Tempest, The (Shakespeare), 36
Texas, 91-103, 122
Themba, Can, 8, 10-12, 194; "Mob Passion," 12-13; "Passionate Stranger," 11
Theroux, Paul, 29

Thoughts Abroad (Bruin [Brutus]), 97-99
"Tiger's Empire, The" (Ogunde), 151
Time, 121, 170
To Felix with Love (Kalitera), 86
To Ndirande Mountain with Love (Kalitera), 79, 86-87
Tonyenvadji, Mr., 153
"Towards Liberty" (Ogunde), 151
Townsend, Rev. Henry, 118
Transformation, 111, 113
Transition, 44, 46
Traveling theatre, 145, 174
Trials of Lumumba, Jomo Kenyatta and St. Paul, The, 108
Trinidad, 181
Troilus, 63
"Troilus and Criseyde" (Chaucer), 63
Troubadour Press, 96-98
True Confessions of "Folake," The, 108
Trust No-body in Time Because Human Being is Trickish and Difficult, 109
Tse-tung, Mao, 101-02
Tsotsis, 12
Turner, Darwin T., 40
Tutuola, Amos, 26, 73; *Ajaiyi and His Inherited Poverty*, 32; "Ajaiyi and the Witchdoctor," 32; *The Palm-Wine Drinkard*, 23
TV Times and Radio News, 146

U Tam'si, Tchicaya, 28
Ufahamu, 98
Uganda, 39, 43
Ugonna, Nnabuenyi, 39
Uka, Kalu, 173
Umodzi, 50
Unibadan traveling theatre, 174
Unife Theatre, 158-84
Union of African Performing Artists News, 51
Union of Nigerian Dramatists and Playwrights, 145
United States of America, 25, 29, 32-33, 37-39, 44-46, 53, 55, 68, 73, 91-92, 94, 97-98, 120-21, 131, 158, 167, 169, 171, 177
University College Ibadan, 43
University Herald, 43
University of: Botswana, 47; California at Los Angeles (UCLA), 91-92; Denver, 94; Ibadan, 43, 158, 169; Ife, 47, 158-84; Lagos, 38, 158, 172; Malawi, 49-51, 75; Nairobi, 47; Nigeria, Nsukka, 29, 44, 47; Port Harcourt, 47, 183; Sierra Leone, 38, 47; Texas at

Austin, 92-102; Texas System, 94; Yaoundé, 51; Zimbabwe, 47; Zululand, 47
"Ut Omnes Unum Sint?" (Armah), 58-59
Uwaifo, Victor, 172

"Vengeance is Mine," 6
Vesey, Paul, 25-26
Vincent, Theo, 40
Voice, The (Okara), 32
"Voter, The" (Achebe), 32

Wachuku, Dr. Jaja, 120
Walcott, Derek, Dream on Monkey Mountain, 176
Walk in the Night, A (La Guma), 18
Wannenburgh, Alf, 28
Wapangwa, 29
Wasimi African School, Ijebu Ode, 154
Watergate, 121
Way to Get Money: The Best Wonderful Book for Money Mongers, The, 108
Weimar Theatre, 167
Wenger, Susanne, 23, 27, 31
West Africa, 29-30, 33-34, 37
West African Higher School Certificate, 54, 66
West African Pilot, 121
West Indians, 23, 25-30, 32-33, 37, 181

West Regional Government, Nigeria, 120
Western Hemisphere, 91
Western Nigeria, 155
Western State, Nigeria, 154
Why Are We So Blest? (Armah), 53, 63
Why Father Why (Kalitera), 79, 83-85, 87-89
Why Son Why (Kalitera), 86, 89
Wilkov, A., 6, 194
Williams, Tennessee, 19
Woman in Her Prime, A (Konadu), 35
Wonodi, Okogbule, 29
Work in Progress, 49, 51
Working Papers in African Literature, 49
World Black Arts Festival, 155
World Congress of Black Writers and Artists, 23-24
Woyengi (Beier), 31
Wren, Robert, 39
Wright, Derek, 53, 69, 194
Wright, Richard, 19; Black Power, 23
Writers Workshop (Ife), 47
Writers' Workshop (Zomba), 50
"Writing a Novel" (Fagunwa), 137-40
Wylie, Hal, 99

Yale University, 171

Yeyemi (Ogunde), 155
Yoruba: community, 155;
    culture, 180; gods, 182;
    language, 118, 152, 155,
    180; literature, 31, 74, 137;
    myths, 26, 31; names, 180;
    novel, 35; operatic
    theatre, 145; people, 118;
    poetry, 23; poets, 37;
    proverbs, 35;
    pseudonym, 31; traveling
    theatre, 145
"Yoruba Ronu" (Ogunde),
    155
Yorubaland, 30, 180
"Yours Forever" (Ogunde),
    151

Zambia, 133
Zaria, Nigeria, 152
Zeleza, Paul, 50
Zimbabwe, 40
Zomba, Malawi, 49
Zonk, 6
Zuka, 44

49 Wise Sayings, 72 Idioms, 44
    Questions and Answers and
    Some Speeches of World
    Leaders Past and Present
    (Abiakam), 111